A Democracy of Ghosts

Poetic Patterns of Mexican-American Life

Anthony Koeninger

KENDALL/HUNT PUBLISHING COMPANY
4050 Westmark Drive   Dubuque, Iowa 52002

Books by Anthony Koeninger

Feast of November, Vol. I   [1990]

Feast of November, Vol. II   [1990]

Gaviota   [1991]

Poems for Bessie Smith   [1992]

Poems for Billie Holiday   [1993]

Pieces of Blue   [1993]

An Overview of America (with Curtis B. Solberg)   [1993]

A People's Heritage (with Curtis B. Solberg and David Morris)   [2000]

Waiting for Preceding Spirits   [2002]

Farming the Moonlight   [2004]

A Democracy of Ghosts   [2007]

The Silent Kingdoms of Memory   [2007]

Copyright © 2007 by Anthony Sean Koeninger

ISBN 10: 0-7575-4143-7
ISBN 13: 978-0-7575-4143-8

Printed in the United States of America

10   9   8   7   6   5   4   3   2   1

For my Grandmother, Mae C. Silverberg

[April 2, 1900-March 23, 2000]

For my Mother, Rebecca Ellen Koeninger

[March 12, 1939-February 11, 2005]

Birds of paradise droop their heads in sorrow,
    rain clouds fill their eyes.

I tell them to lift their heads to the heavens
so that the wind—your spirits—
can brush their faces.

I love you, my dear Grandma, I adore you, my beloved Mom,
now
and to the end of time.

CONTENTS

A luminous glow   117

A democracy of ghosts   205

The continuing story of Guadalupe and Quetzalcóatl   257

ACKNOWLEDGMENTS

None of these poems would have been written without the encouragement given to me by mother, Rebecca Ellen Koeninger, and from my grandmother, Mae C. Silverberg. I am eternally indebted to them. The poet fails to find the right words.

I have a special debt to Kendall-Hunt Publishing Company's Senior Editor Joe Wells, who guided the manuscript to completion. I have also been fortunate in having Victoria Bursey, English professor at Cuesta College, to edit many of the poems as they progressed through various drafts.

A special acknowledgment must also be extended to my feline companions who have blessed my life over the last forty years: Thomas, Felix I, Felixtess I, Felixtess II, Kelly, Felixtess III, Grapes I, Felixtess IV, Sunshine, Felix II, Grapes II, Grapes III, Felixtess V, and Felixtess VI. Their loving, playful, cantankerous, inquisitive, mysterious personalities have enriched me with endless joy.

Please watch over me, Rebecca and Mae, and guide me home to you.

Anthony Sean Koeninger
El Rancho de las Gatas de Dios,
Atascadero, California
March 12, 2007

Dearest Anthony
May you always find the peace and comfort
you seek from The Faith you have in your heart
and the light which comes from your soul.

WITH ALL MY LOVE,

MOM

CHRISTMAS 1992

With what gift shall I come into the Lord's presence
and bow down before God on High?
This is what the Lord requires of you: only this,
to act justly,
to love faithfully
and to walk humbly with your God.

—MICAH 6:6, 8

A poem dealing with history is no more at liberty to violate what the writer takes to be the spirit of history than it is at liberty to violate what he takes to be the nature of the human heart.

★ ROBERT PENN WARREN

The statements ascribed to the historical figures in these poems are based on the letters, diaries, addresses, and documents of the time. All non-historical figures are identified as fictional in the footnotes.

A Democracy of Ghosts

The people commonly called "Aztecs" called themselves "Mexica" (pronounced: meh-SHEE-kah). The Spanish conquistadores, friars, and chroniclers did not use the designation "Aztecs," a term that was first popularized by the Spanish Jesuit Father Francisco Javier Clavijero in the eighteenth century and by U.S. historian William H. Prescott and German naturalist Alexander von Humboldt in the nineteenth century.

The Mexica may have used the name "Azteca" (meaning "People of Aztlán") in the thirteenth century during their migration from their ancestral homeland, but, according to Mexica theology, they renamed themselves "Mexica" at the insistence of their god Huitzilopochtli.

The Mexica kings

Acamapichtli   1375-1395
Huitzilíhuitl   1396-1417
Chimalpopoca   1417-1426
Itzcóatl   1427-1440
Motecuhzoma Ilhuicamina   1440-1469
Axayácatl   1469-1481
Tizoc   1481-1486
Ahuítzotl   1486-1502
Motecuhzoma Xocoyotzin   1502-1520
Cuitláhuac   1520
Cuauhtémoc   1520-1525

In our sleep, we may recall the days beyond memory

In the beginning,
all was sky, a blue void,
and even the gods had no home.

As our lords wandered across the face of the heavens,
they set the stars on fire, one after another,
weaving light into darkness.

In the splendor of the first sun,
the gods made a home for themselves in still canyons.

Time was frozen in jade, in solid green moon.
There was no movement, no breath.
All was still.

And then the gods made motion,
and made time move.

In those first days beyond memory,
our blessed lords made wind from stillness,
coaxed light from darkness.

Our gods made a kingdom for themselves
among reed and snake,
heron and dispersing waters.

Finally, the gods blew life into dust,
and then man was.

The serpent with brilliant feathers

Quetzalcóatl's eyes glow like obsidian.
His chalky, bearded face emerges from a bouquet of feathers.
White curved teeth protrude from open jaws.
His serpent body undulates in the heavens.

Our feathered serpent killed darkness, killed flatness,
as he lifted the sky high above the earth.

He descended into the place where no smoke escapes
to bring forth mortal bones
brought to life by his own blood.

Praise to lord Quetzalcóatl, bearer of corn,
revealer of all learning,
who brought forth stone carvings and calendars
from the silence of his mind.

Truly with him it began—
truly from him it flowed out,
all art and knowledge.

Who is more esteemed than Quetzalcóatl?
Who is more adored than he?
Never can his name be lost.

The most beautiful singing birds accompany the plumed serpent
wherever he goes. Surely those florescent birds are singing to him now.

Oh, Quetzalcóatl, our precious snake,

when you sailed away to the east on your raft of serpents
you made a sunset of our hearts.

When will you come back from the sunrise to the place of your throne?

Until then, we lament with hearts of shattered jade.

Quetzalcóatl: (pronounced: Keht-sahl-coh'-atl) Mexica creator god and priestly figure. Quetzalcóatl's name means feathered snake, or, plumed serpent. **His chalky, bearded face:** Quetzalcóatl was depicted as light-skinned and bearded, the only Mexica god who had a human face and body. Quetzalcóatl forbade human sacrifice and preached a peaceful existence, demanding only the sacrifice of serpents and butterflies in his name. Beginning under the *huei tlatoani* (great speaker, or king) Itzcóatl (r.1427-1440), the Mexica magnified the status of Huitzilopochtli, the god of war and lord of the sun. In stark contrast to Quetzalcóatl, Huitzilopochtli demanded the sacrifice of human hearts in his name. The Mexica believed that human sacrifice placated Huitzilopochtli and kept the sun moving across the sky. **he lifted the heavens:** Quetzalcóatl was the lifter of the heavens and the revealer of the earth with its hills, fertile soil, and waters. The combination of the tropical quetzal bird and the snake coupled the celestial and terrestrial spheres and symbolized creativity and fertility to the Mexica. **He descended into the place where no smoke escapes to bring forth mortal bones:** Quetzalcóatl descended into the netherworld, Mictlán, The Place of the Dead, or, literally, the Dead Below. He absconded from the underworld with the bones of humans. He then passed a thorn through his penis to shed his blood on the bones, creating human life. Quetzalcóatl was the patron of the Toltec and Mexica priesthoods. To demonstrate piety or as an act of penitence, Mexica priests passed a sharpened bone, obsidian, reed, thorn, or maguey spine through an ear lobe, nose, tongue or penis to sacrifice blood in emulation of Quetzalcóatl. **bearer of corn:** After the gods had hidden corn inside a magic mountain, Quetzalcóatl turned himself into an ant. He entered the mountain and obtained kernels of corn, which he gave to humans. As a result, Quetzalcóatl was celebrated as the bearer of corn. **revealer of all learning:** Quetzalcóatl had multiple aspects: He created arts and crafts, music, and was the father of stone engraving. Quetzalcóatl was the inventor of architecture, agriculture, song, sculpture, metallurgy, and jewelry. He was the revealer of all learning. A Mexica prayer proclaimed: "Truly with him it began, truly from him it flowed out, from Quetzalcóatl—all art and knowledge." It was said that only through poetry, music, and art could one truly understand Quetzalcóatl. Even with the intense Mexica devotion to Huitzilopochtli and Tezcatlipoca, Quetzalcóatl remained an indispensable source of inspiration and sanctification in Mexica society. Many temples were erected in his honor. The god carried with him a priestly incense pouch so that he could cense, and make sacred, the things of the earth. Quetzalcóatl's piety—as historian Burr Cartwright Brundage wrote—was intense and elitist; only the most dedicated, sanctified priests could emulate the plumed serpent. **Never can your name be lost:** these words are from a Mexica song lamenting Quetzalcóatl's exile. **The most beautiful singing birds accompany the plumed serpent wherever he goes:** Quetzalcóatl held the secret of all enchantments. Beautiful singing birds traveled with him on his journeys. **Oh, Quetzalcóatl, our precious snake, when you sailed away to the east on your raft of serpents you made a sunset of our hearts:** Quetzalcóatl's bitter arch-rival was Tezcatlipoca (pronounced: Tehs-cah-tlee-poh'cah), the god of night and material things. Tezcatlipoca's name means, "Smoking Mirror." Tezcatlipoca's mirror gave off dense smoke and killed enemies. His smoking mirror also gave him a window on the entire world. The dark-skinned and eternally young Tezcatlipoca was well versed in sorcery, and was eager to use his skills as a sorcerer to mischievous ends. He was a tempter, urging men to do evil. Tezcatlipoca and Quetzalcóatl were complete opposites in many ways, but especially in the fact that Tezcatlipoca represented darkness and Quetzalcóatl represented light. Also, Tezcatlipoca represented material things while Quetzalcóatl symbolized spirituality.

Tezcatlipoca was deeply envious and provoked by the love and affection that mortals lavished upon Quetzalcóatl—the gentle god of creation and peace. So Tezcatlipoca and the other nefarious gods of the netherworld presented the austere Quetzalcóatl with a gift concealed in cotton wrapping. It was a mirror in which the feathered serpent saw that he had a human face, and, perhaps, a human destiny. Quetzalcóatl was aghast by this revelation. Exasperated by Quetzalcóatl's "irritating purity," Tezcatlipoca prepared an intoxicating potion consisting of *pulque* (the fermented juice of the maguey cactus) that he hoped the feathered serpent would drink, thus corrupting him and preventing him from performing his sacraments. Deeply despairing after he had gazed into Tezcatlipoca's mirror, Quetzalcóatl drank heavily and fornicated. In the morning, Quetzalcóatl was stricken with disgust and overwhelming sorrow as he realized that he had been enticed by the nefarious Tezcatlipoca into violating his priestly vows of sobriety and sexual abstinence. Quetzalcóatl believed that he had lost his piety and his moral authority. The humiliated Quetzalcóatl fled on a sea-going raft of serpents, sailing in the direction of the sunrise. He promised to return in the year Ce Acatl (1-Reed) to reclaim his rule and see if men and women had taken care of the earth in his absence. Quetzalcóatl prophesied the annihilation of the world on the day 4-Ollin (the Day of Movement, which referred to an earthquake). He promised the creation of a new world and a new reign of justice and prosperity.

Quetzalcóatl arrived on the celestial shore of divine waters, where he wept profusely. He discarded his fabulous ornaments, green mask, and resplendent feathers. In deep remorse, he then sacrificed himself by cremation. The smoke from his burning body became the Morning Star while birds in the colors of the rainbow emerged from the ashes of his funeral pyre. Quetzalcóatl's promised return filled the native world with premonition about future events. When would the great Quetzalcóatl return to sit in judgment? When would the world end? To the present day there are people in Mexico who believe that Quetzalcoátl will yet return in a spectacular manifestation to judge mankind and to transform the present times and modern world into an idyllic past. **When will you come back from the sunrise to the place of your throne?:** from a Mexica prayer in remembrance of Quetzalcóatl: "He will come back to the place of his throne for that is what he promised when he departed."

Lord of the smoking mirror

His head is encircled with a band of burnished gold
ending in golden ears.
His face is painted with puffs of smoke.

Tezcatlipoca was born among jaguars and obsidian.
Born when darkness still ruled,
he lives in darkness still.

He blots out the blue sky with black ink,
obscures the sun in smoke.

He turns birds into silence and silence into thunder.

Tezcatlipoca, lord of the smoking mirror,
ministers in dark heavens.
He is lord of the slain stars,
lord of mockeries and metamorphoses,
lord of affliction and anguish.

This lord is the skunk,
the vulture that laughs like a man.
He is the bundle of ashes,
an apparition of the dead.

Tezcatlipoca descends from the night skies,
crouching vigilant in the heaving wind.
He moves among thieves carrying knives;
he makes the sky rain stones.

How adroitly he twists fate,

tempts men into darkness.

Tezcatlipoca places us in the palm of his hand.
He makes us round.
We roll, we become pellets.
He casts us from side to side.

He makes a mockery of us.
We make him laugh.

Willful and mercurial,
dark, bloodied, brooding,
he is a shadow, always slinking away.

His sorcerers, harnessed to smoke,
make omens dance in the opaque sky.

These wizards hurl maladies and phantasms across the land,
while Tezcatlipoca, the jaguar,
annihilates all that he wants to annihilate.

Tezcatlipoca: (pronounced: Tehs-cah-tlee-poh'cah) the god of the night sky and material things, whose name means "Smoking Mirror," from the Náhuatl, *tezcatl,* meaning mirror and *poca,* which means to emit smoke. Tezcatlipoca was dark-skinned, eternally young, and fickle. He was associated with destiny; in fact, he was the very embodiment of the unpredictability of fate and capricious power. Tezcatlipoca was identified with wind and night, suggesting the breath of life, mystery, invincibility, and pervasiveness. He was the taker of life; his laughter signaled destruction. He was the lord of sorcerers, who mischievously transformed shapes. As significantly, Tezcatlipoca's enormous power was especially identified with the Mexica royalty. Tezcatlipoca was a patron deity to the Mexica kings. Sovereigns received their power to rule, reward, and punish through the auspices of Tezcatlipoca. The Mexica kings were Tezcatlipoca's vicars on earth. They had a sacred obligation to rule wisely and morally because, through Tezcatlipoca's power as god of punitive justice, the kings were empowered with the "fangs and claws of justice." Indeed, a Mexica king ruled at Tezcatlipoca's pleasure; at any time, for any reason, the god with the smoking mirror could depose the king. Accordingly, upon his election, the Mexica *tlatoani* (speaker, or king), spoke directly to Tezcatlipoca, the patron of rulers "who had been born and sanctified in signs and constellations under which lords are born, to be your instruments and images, to preside over your kingdoms, you being within them and speaking with their lips, they pronouncing your words." Tezcatlipoca gave men prayer as a means to communicate with the gods. Many of the sacred prayers in the rites of Mexica kingship were recited in Tezcatlipoca's honor. All members of Mexica society confessed sins to Tezcatlipoca through the intercession of soothsayers and priests. During rites of confession, the god's name was invoked with a litany of titles in petitions that were solemnly uttered. After the confessor enumerated his transgressions, he was mandated to do penance by fasting. Sometimes a penitent was told to perform a blood sacrifice by piercing a tongue or ears with a reed or maguey spine. In honor of Tezcatlipoca, the Mexica lit lamps or fires inside their temples. In his 1993 book, *Conquest: Montezuma, Cortés, and the Fall of Old Mexico,* Hugh Thomas wrote: "Wherever [Tezcatlipoca] appeared on earth, he caused confusion. He was an arbitrary god. But he also stood for total power. At the same time, by one of those perplexing double identifications so favored by the Mexica, he was also the eternally youthful warrior, the patron of the military academy, of the royal family, who could bring wealth, heroism, valor, dignity, rulership, nobility, and honor." The Spanish priest and historian Fray Bernardino de Sahagún recorded a far more negative perspective on Tezcatlipoca. Within a generation of the Spanish conquest of Mexico, Sahagún wrote: [T]hey say that [Tezcatlipoca] disrupted all peace and friendship and that he created enmity and hatred among people and kings. And it is not surprising that he should do it on earth as he had already done it in heaven, as it is written in Holy Scriptures. . . This is the evil Lucifer, father of all meanness and lies, very embittered and proud, who tricked your ancestors." **His head is encircled with a band of burnished gold ending in golden ears:** from a Spanish description of a statue of Tezcatlipoca. The Mexica often portrayed Tezcatlipoca as a warrior armed with a spear, arrows, and shield. His body and limbs were always painted black, while his face was tinged with gold, with three black stripes, one over his brow, one across his nose, and one on his chin. In Mexica depictions, Tezcatlipoca wears the double heron feathers of Mexica warriors in his hair with a tall-feathered back piece tied to his body. **Born when darkness still ruled:** Tezcatlipoca was born before the gods created light. **with black ink:** Tezcatlipoca was inextricably identified with blackness and nighttime. The Mexica often crafted images of him from shiny black obsidian, and those men who served in the priesthood of Tezcatlipoca painted their faces in a heavy paste of black soot. Many Mexica sacred hymns were addressed to Tezcatlipoca. An example follows: "With black ink you will blot out all that was friendship, brotherhood, nobility. You give shading to those who must live on the earth." These prayers lionized Tezcatlipoca's power and urged his compassion in meting out punishment. **the smoking mirror:** The god wore two mirrors on his body, one was an ornament in his hair and another was used as a replacement for a severed foot. In his black obsidian-divining mirror, Tezcatlipoca could see everything that happened in the world. The divinity held the title Tezcatlanextia, which means "He Who Causes Things to Be Seen in the Mirror." Indeed, the fates of mortals were reflected in his mirrored glass. The god could transform himself into a monkey, jaguar, skunk, coyote, or turkey so that he could study the behavior of men. He amused himself in his numerous metamorphoses. He was the Mexica deity who constantly interacted with mortals. Tezcatlipoca "mocked and ridiculed men," was a provoker of vice and sin, and "brought all things down." In any one of his disparate forms, Tezcatlipoca during the day haunted crossroads, which the Mexica believed to be places of peril and ill fortune. Not only was Tezcatlipoca able to observe and affect mortal behavior, he was the only Mexica deity empowered with prevision; he had divine instruments (perhaps in addition to his oracular mirror) that gave him the gift of clairvoyance. Tezcatlipoca carried arrows to inflict punishment on those who he had seduced to commit wrongdoing or flagrant acts of evil. His enormous power, capricious nature, and omniscience filled people with fear and awe. The Mexica made innumerable representations of the Lord of the Smoking Mirror on animal skins and stones. During the annual feast of Tezcatlipoca, an *ixiptla* (a representative or image of divinity) walked through the streets of Tenochtitlán (pronounced: tay-noch-tee-TLAHN), the Mexica capital, playing a clay flute, smoking, and smelling flowers. Observers bowed to Tezcatlipoca's *ixiptla,* the human surrogate, and kissed the earth in a sign of respect. At the end of the festival, the *ixiptla,* always a handsome young male, was sacrificed. **lord of the slain stars:** Tezcatlipoca was born fully dressed as a warrior, wielding sacrificial obsidian knives. His first act was the destruction of the stars. He was one of the divinities who protected Mexica warriors in battle. **lord of mockeries and metamorphoses:** from Guilhem Olivier's 2003 title, *Mockeries and Metamorphoses of an Mexica God: Tezcatlipoca, "Lord of the Smoking Mirror."* In addition to his heron feathers, mirrors, back tie, black and gold paint, Tezcatlipoca was crowned with the starry diadem of the night sky. But he was also saddled with a wooden collar around his neck, a symbol of subordination that was worn by slaves and prisoners of war. During the annual feast day of Tezcatlipoca, Mexica nobles unfastened the restraining collars of their slaves, who then welcomed and feasted throughout the god's festivity day. Failure to treat slaves as honored guests during that celebratory day could bring Tezcatlipoca's wrath, reducing an affluent noble to destitution and slavery. Even Tezcatlipoca himself was not immune to irony and mockery since, as Burr Cartwright Brundage wrote, "only the intensity of Mexica belief in him prevented this excess [of reverence] from degenerating into caricature and effrontery." **the vulture that laughs like a man:** Tezcatlipoca also used a bird guise, the vulture, considered by the Mexica to be a creature of ill-omen. The Florentine Codex described vultures that "laugh like men." **He is the bundle of ashes, an apparition of the dead:** Besides his animal guises, Tezcatlipoca assumed a host of horrible appearances to terrify people: a decapitated man with his chest split open, a funerary bundle of ashes, a giant, and a groaning corpse. Tezcatlipoca's hideous apparitions exhibited the demonic aspect of his nature. **he makes the sky rain stones:** hailstones. **Tezcatlipoca places us in the palm of his hand:** a Mexica description of Tezcatlipoca recorded in The Florentine Codex. **he is a shadow, always slinking away:** from Olivier, *Mockeries and Metamorphoses.* **maladies:** in this instance, infectious diseases. **Tezcatlipoca, the jaguar, annihilates all that he wants to annihilate:** Tezcatlipoca was often associated with the ferocious jaguar. In fact, the jaguar was Tezcatlipoca's preferred animal double. The historian Burr Cartwright Brundage argued that the link between Tezcatlipoca, the gifted sorcerer, and the jaguar was a natural one because of the animal's remarkable night vision, strength, and stealth. A Mexica scribe, interviewed by the Spanish Catholic priest and historian Fray Bernardino de Sahagún, praised the ferocious feline: "It is a dweller of the forests, of crags, of water; noble, princely, it is said. It is the lord, the ruler of animals. It is cautious, wise, proud. It is not a scavenger. It is one which detests, which is nauseated by dirty things. It is noble, proud. . . . And by night it watches; it seeks out what it hunts, which it eats. In truth, it sees very well; it can see far. Even if it is very dark, even if it is misty, it sees." The spotted pelt of the jaguar was significant in Mexica symbolism; it represented the stars in the night sky and coincided with the feline's nocturnal activities.

Aztlán

The magicians gather amid flocks of heron, white as chalk,
swirling like pale dust in the skies over Aztlán,
the sacred land of the ancestors,
the birthplace of our god, Huitzilopochtli.

The magicians bathe themselves in their good luck.
They make beautiful symbols in the wet earth
among countless reeds and rushes.

The heads of these wizards are still as death,
but their tongues flicker like the tongues of snakes
and their eyes glow like a fire anguishing on the moon.

The sorcerers sing their incantations,
sanctifying the earth of Aztlán.

These wizards throw their eyes into future days,
and offer a solitary forecast:
Though jade be broken and the bravest jaguars die,
Aztlán, our holy home, will live always in the painted poems
and the scent of magnificent flowers.

We are water splashed on stone,
but Aztlán will have no end.

Aztlán: About four hundred years before the arrival of the Europeans in the Western hemisphere, the Mexica migrated to a great valley in central Mexico. The Mexica migrated from the north, from their homeland called Aztlán (pronounced: Ahst-lan)—which means "Place of the White Herons," or "Place of Whiteness." The location of Aztlán is the subject of scholarly debate. Some Mexican-Americans say that Aztlán was located in what is now the southwestern United States, perhaps around the Salton Sea in southern California or sprawled along the banks of the Colorado River. Others say it was in northern Mexico—in the area of Zacatecas (or Nayarit). Yet other scholars say that Aztlán was only the mythical home of the Mexica people. Meanwhile, historians have studied Mexica historical chronicles and the Mexica calendar—and correlated that data with the Christian calendar—and calculated that the Mexica began their exodus from Aztlán in the twelfth century. Beginning in 1298(?), the Mexica migrants occupied Chapultepec, a hill that overlooks today's Mexico City from the west, before being driven out of the area. Then, after a period spent in servitude in Culhuacán, south of modern Mexico City, the Mexica founded Tenochtitlán (pronounced: tay-noch-tee-TLAHN), their great city, in 1325 (the Mexica year 2-House). **Huitzilopochtli:** (pronounced: Weet-zeel-oh-póhsh-tlee) Mexica god of the sun and war. Please see the poem "Huitzilopochtli, in the beginning and in the end."

The people nobody wishes to see

The Mexica wander nomadically without faces.

They gather dried and prickly fruits in a fitful sun,
praying in murmurous cadences to menacing gods.

They move from barren place to desolation,
from sun to moon, leaving relics and treasures
buried in the desert wilderness.

Their sacred effigies and shards of visions speak silently
to the heart of the earth.

Their pots and stone tools lay scattered.

The Mexica dress as mean animals scattered in starlight.

In the great valley of Metzico
nobody wishes to receive them,
these barbarians,
the last people to come.

But the blessed priests crowded in the shadows
study obscure etchings on maguey fiber.

They alone glimpse the strange nights burning under future moons.

They see an aura around kings not yet born.

In the great valley of Metzico / nobody wishes to receive them, / these barbarians, / the last people to come: According to Mexica chronicles, the Mexica were despised by the established settlers in the central valley. The Mexica were derided as "the last people to come." It was said that "everyone persecuted them," "no one wished to receive them," "they had no face" and that they were "uncouth" and "barbarians." But the Mexica would rise to become the most powerful people in Mexico, creating one of the great civilizations in world history. **Metzico:** an alternate pronunciation of Mexico.

Tenochtitlán

The implacable god Huitzilopochtli snarls like a wounded jaguar
burning in the sun.

His wrath is old, and deep as sound.
His dimmest dreams are law.

Huitzilopochtli's children gather on an island of reeds
rustling with snakes that rattle in the wind.

Tenoch, dressed in the white robe of authority,
points to the tall cactus where the eagle stands,
with its wings stretched out towards the rays of the sun.
The majestic bird gathers its heat in the coolness of the morning
and in its beak and claw writhe a very elegant serpent.

Here is the place where we, the Mexica, the chosen people of the Sun,
will raise our city, Tenochtitlán,
the place where the eagle screams,
the place where the fishes swim,
Tenochtitlán!

Tenochtitlán: (pronounced: tay-noch-tee-TLAHN) the capital of the Mexica empire.
Huitzilopochtli: the Mexica god of war and lord of the sun. **Tenoch:** (d.?1376) Tenoch
reportedly was the foremost of four priest-rulers, or bearers of the god Huitzilopochtli,
during the Mexicas' first decades at Tenochtitlán. The name Tenochtitlán is sometimes
translated as "Place Founded by Tenoch." Scholars debate whether Tenoch was a
mythological figure or an actual Mexica leader who was later mythologized. **the tall
cactus where the eagle stands:** Huitzilopochtli commanded the Mexica to abandon
the ancestral birthplace, Aztlán, and search for a new homeland where they would dis-
cover an eagle with a snake in its beak, and that the eagle would be perched on a tall
nopal cactus growing forth from a rock. The lines in the final two stanzas come from an
actual Mexica chronicle recording the founding of the new Mexica homeland at
Tenochtitlán, in 1325 (the Mexica year 2-House). The *Codex Ramírez* records that the
majestic eagle bowed its head as the Mexica approached its resting place atop the nopal
cactus. The newcomers immediately prostrated themselves before the eagle, snake, and

cactus, overcome with happiness, knowing that their arduous wandering was over. According to their theology, the Mexica were commanded by Huitzilopochtli to remain at Tenochtitlán until their world ended. **the chosen people of the Sun:** during the long migration from Aztlán to Tenochtitlán, the Mexica had come to see themselves as a messianic people. According to Mexica theology, Huitzilopochtli had told the migrants from Aztlán: "Wander, look for lands. . .send pioneers ahead, have them plant maize, when the harvest is ready, move up to it—keep me, Huitzilopochtli, always with you, carrying me like a banner, feed me on human hearts torn from the recently sacrificed."

She speaks thunderously

She orders the inferior men sent away.

Ilancueitl prays to the goddesses
for flashes of wisdom.

She speaks thunderously of the alignment of stars
that have figured prominently in the calamities of the past.

This queen has a window on the fates
and she will not be suppressed.

No man will suppress her.

She orders the inferior men sent away: Some scholars argue that Mexica men and women played different—but equivalent—roles. They argue that women were nearly the equals of men. Women cared for children and transmitted Mexica culture and traditions to them. But women played important roles in Mexica society, beyond the roles of mothers and wives. Some women entered the priesthood and became priestesses. The main function of women priests was to teach girls in the schools. Mexica women participated in the economy as merchants, traders, and producers. Women made ceramic pots, wove cloths, and cooked tortillas and tamales for sale in the marketplace. Some upper class Mexica women owned property. But other scholars assert that Mexica society was rigidly male-centered and male-dominated. These scholars claim that as Mexica society became increasingly militaristic, men became increasingly powerful. These historians argue that Mexica culture can be described as puritanical, militaristic, and paternalistic. A preponderance of evidence indicates that women were subservient to men. An anthropologist has written that Mexica men wanted their women "tied to the *comal* [the clay dish] and the preparation of the tortilla." Women were not permitted to enter politics or the military, nor could they become musicians or poets who recited in public. **Ilancueitl:** In some Mexica chronicles and modern histories of the Mexica empire, Ilancueitl ("Old Woman-Skirt") is listed as a queen in her own right (from 1349-1375) and then as a co-ruler (1375-1383) with her husband, King Acamapichtli. In fact, some texts identify Ilancueitl as the "Founding Queen" of the Tenochca. The Culhuacán royal woman, Ilancueitl, brought the Tolteca lineage of Culhuacán (also Colhuacán) to Tenochtitlán, allowing the Mexica kings to claim a direct descent from the revered Tolteca culture. Ilancueitl was said to have wielded vast political power during her husband's reign.

The coronation of Acamapichtli

The ancient priest raises his left hand to the Sun
and with his right palm,
smears red oil on Acamapichtli's face.

The priest sprinkles sweet water on the lord's body
and places poems, like plumes, at his feet.

He rests the turquoise diadem, like a blue star,
on the young king's head.

The holy man steps back and bows deeply,
like the moon dropping behind the hills at dawn.

Acamapichtli: (pronounced: Ah-kah-mah-peteh'li) Mexica king, 1375-1395.

Acamapichtli emerges from a luminous darkness

The women, in their ornaments, gather, one after one,
inside the palace,
where incense smoke and the scent of flowers
soak the moonless evening.

These women, barefoot, strangely attired,
keep their silence,
though inside the wells of their hearts
the most wondrous birds sing in the first morning of the world.

In this luxuriant silence, the women wait.

They await their lord, Acamapichtli,
father of the kingdom,
master of flower and song.

Crowned with turquoise diadem and the rays of the sun,
Acamapichtli emerges from a luminous darkness.
He is blessed among the blessed,
content, contemplative,
serene as he sits upon the royal mat.
The women wash his face and hands, and shape his hair into pillars of stone.

There is quiet inside Tenochtitlán,
but, with each full moon burning audaciously among the map of stars,
every sort of prized and priceless good flows from the city,
in tribute, to the lordly Tepaneca.

Acamapichtli's people, the Mexica, many of them, weep
as they deliver ducks, frogs, and fish,

juniper berries and willow leaves into the hands of foreign masters.

These memories, each one a sour seed, will blossom
into something both beautiful and dreadful.

Acamapichtli: (pronounced: Ah-kah-mah-peteh'li) Mexica king, 1375-1395. Acamapichtli was the son of a Mexica nobleman and a Culhuacan princess. He was also a descendent of the original Mexica immigrants from Aztlán. His name means "Handful of Reeds." Acamapichtli's primary wife was Ilancueitl (please see the poem, "She speaks thunderously"). He had no children with her, but he did father several sons, and possibly many daughters as well, by his twenty other wives. **flower and song:** the combined Mexica symbols for poetry. **turquoise diadem:** the symbol of the Mexica kingship. It was known to the Mexica as the turquoise diadem of Tonacatecuhtli, who was the lord of abundance, the lord of the fertility of men and the earth, and the measurer of time. **sits upon the royal mat:** the woven reed mat upon which the Mexica king sat was a symbol of royal power and privilege. **shape his hair into pillars of stone:** In Mexica sacred books, Acamapichtli's hair was arranged to represent pillars of stone. In turn, the pillars symbolized valiant performance in battle. **There is quiet inside Tenochtitlán:** According to the Spanish historian Fray Bernardino de Sahagún, there was "peace and quiet" in Tenochtitlán (pronounced: Tay-noch-tee-TLAHN), the Mexica capital, during Acamapichtli's reign. **every sort of prized and priceless good flows from the city, in tribute, to the lordly Tepaneca:** During their early years at Tenochtitlán, the Mexica were tributary subjects of the powerful Tepaneca empire. Every full moon, the Mexica were required to deliver products from Lake Texcoco to Tepaneca rulers. **Acamapichtli's people, the Mexica, many of them, weep / as they deliver ducks, frogs, and fish, / juniper berries and willow leaves into the hands of foreign masters:** Many of the old Mexica drawings depict the people of Tenochtitlán weeping as they delivered their tributary goods to the Tepanecas. **These memories, each one a sour seed:** According to some accounts, Acamapichtli barely had enough to eat and died grieving that he had not been able to free the Mexica from their tributary obligations to the Tepanecas. Many years after Acamapichtli's reign, the memories of their subordination drove the Mexica to acquire imperial power.

Acamapichtli's flesh is brown like dried mud

Acamapichtli sits placid, inscrutable,
like a great stone idol
perched on the woven mat of kings.
He is still as silence; unflinching
and unflinchable.
His flesh is brown like dried mud,
his muscles, sunned rock.
The turquoise diadem with red back-tie
shimmers like the morning star on his head.
His eyes are seas of fire smoldering like gasping suns.
Every word lingers in his heart,
none pass from his lips.
Finally, the king bows his head in contemplation,
a deep and lasting prayer
that cajoles the birds to fly from his head.

Acamapichtli: Mexica king, 1375-1395. Acamapichtli was elected king, or *tlatoani* (speaker) of the Mexica at the age of twenty. Under Acamapichtli, the Mexica, not yet risen to imperial power, fought as mercenaries in the military campaigns of the powerful Tepaneca empire. Even during those early engagements, the Mexica distinguished themselves as reliable and valiant soldiers. The most significant campaign was waged against Chalco, a town on the eastern shore of Lake Texcoco, beginning in 1395 and continuing intermittently over the next twelve years. While his subjects were essentially vassals of the Tepanecas, Acamapichtli focused his royal duties on the construction of housing complexes, a network of canals and pedestrian walkways, and chinampas (sometimes described as floating gardens of fruits and vegetables) in Lake Texcoco. **woven mat of kings:** Mexica kings sat on a mat of woven reeds, the equivalent of a European throne. **turquoise diadem with red back-tie:** symbols of high office.

Acamapichtli leaves the world

Who are these ghosts who have already
won the kingdom?

What do they know
about distant days,
or the judgments that will soothe or torment us?

Why do these souls stalk us
when we only seek silence in our dying days?

Acamapichtli leaves the world: a reference to the death, in 1395, of Mexica King Acamapichtli.

Huitzilíhuitl gives his philosophy on the meaning of the stars

The elders gazed at the stars,
those painted stones in the obscure sky,
that cast prophecies across the earth.

Look upon those squares of distant light
to see the gods in them,
and even the dying aura of extinguished cities.

The stars that reign like princes in the heavens
keep fate and memory
enshrined in their magical light.

Huitzilíhuitl: (pronounced: Weet-see-lee-weetle) reigned as king of the Mexica from 1396 to 1417. His name means "Hummingbird Feather."

The direct line from the gods to the king

Huitzilíhuitl draws a line from the deities
to his right hand:
>   he raises jagged temples from salt water
and scrawls laws into the sacred books.

In his hands, power increases, perceptibly, day after day,
while animals grow fatter and crops thicken.

The cranes sing in the canals of Tenochtitlán.
Their songs burn across memory, across eternity.

Huitzilíhuitl says that the gods have grown the stars, like flowers,
to spread a glimmering beauty across the darkness.

When the hearts of our kings grow still, like dead copper,
they are woven into that light which burns
only in the night.

Huitzilíhuitl: (pronounced: Weet-see-lee-weetle) reigned as king of the Mexica from 1396 to 1417. His name means "Hummingbird Feather." He was the son of the previous Mexica king, Acamapichtli. **Huitzilíhuitl draws a line from the deities to his right hand:** Mexica royals were expected to maintain dignity. They were to stress duty and deference, self-restraint, temperance, and exercise a rigorous respect for law. When Huitzilíhuitl was enthroned, a delegation representing his subjects said to him: "We give you not rest but work—we have nothing else to give you." **Huitzilíhuitl. . . // raises jagged temples from salt water and scrawls laws into the sacred books:** During Huitzilíhuitl's rulership, people from across the Valley of Mexico settled permanently in Tenochtitlán, the Mexica capital. Huitzilíhuitl devoted himself to constructing temples and shrines in his capital, and codifying laws and social regulations, including prescriptions for honoring the Mexica pantheon of deities and recognizing kings and nobles as the vicars of the gods. Only sixteen years old when he was elected Mexica king, Huitzilíhuitl created a royal council to advise him on matters of state. After Huitzilíhuitl married a daughter of Tepaneca King Tezozómoc, the tribute owed to the Tepanecas was reduced to the symbolic level of two ducks, a few fish and frogs, and other lake products. Huitzilíhuitl committed Mexica warriors to Tepaneca military campaigns that drove towards warm lands, particularly southwards to the Valley of Morelos, and

Cuauhnahuac (Cuernavaca). One of the prizes of the tropical lands was cotton, which Mexica nobles began to wear during Huitzilíhuitl's reign. While it is true that the Mexica played subordinate roles to Tepaneca military commanders and warriors, the junior partnership provided the Mexica with skills in military science and empire building. In addition, the Mexica were given access to the markets of Tepaneca cities. The Mexica continued to provide warriors in Tepeanca wars of conquest during the reign of the next king, Chimalpopoca. Not until Itzcóatl was king, in 1428, were the Mexica able to free themselves from Tepaneca dominance. **from salt water:** the Mexica capital was built on an island in the saline Lake Texcoco. Under Huitzilíhuitl, the Mexica conducted naval warfare drills with canoes.

Smoke mingles with the scent of flowers

One day Quetzalcóatl will come back from his exiled throne
to reclaim his kingdom, ruling again over the painted palaces
and the pyramids of gleaming stucco.

Until the promise is fulfilled,
Huitzilíhuitl, our king, the highest of high priests,
guards the earth for a little while.

He divides the stars among friends and allies,
keeping the oldest lights in the sky
burning at his back.

The descending sun, ascending moon mark time
as the great lords place jades and emeralds in light,
then shadow,
to track the passing of our lives.

Huitzilíhuitl watches his life recede with the sunlight dying
along the length of the causeways.

In his final hours,
Huitzilíhuitl is carried to mountain shrines sheathed in moonlight,
where incense is burnt, smoke rising, dancing,
mingling with the scent of flowers
and the music of drumming and singing
that rise, too, to reach the palaces of the gods.

Our king: Huitzilíhuitl, Mexica king, 1396-1417.

The coronation of Chimalpopoca

The gods of the heavens and the earth
place the boy with eyes round and piercing as stars
on the straw icpalli.

The boy-king, Chimalpopoca, bows his head
as flowery words blossom from the mouths of poets and priests.

A high priest, wearing a cluster of heron feathers on his head,
anoints the king with divine unction,
and places in his left hand, a smoking shield;
in his other, a club armed with obsidian teeth.

The ambassadors from Texcoco and Tlateloco
lower their eyes as the sun bursts into the palace.
They lay liquid amber and strips of gleaming copper
at the feet of the Mexica king.

The musicians blow flutes and conches,
rattling shells and beating drums
as the sun dances upon the earth.

Chimalpopoca: (pronounced: Che-mal-po-po'-ca) reigned as Mexica king from 1417 to 1426. He was ten years old when he ascended to power. **icpalli:** royal mat. **smoking shield; in his other, a club armed with obsidian teeth:** symbols of the war god Huitzilopochtli. Chimalpopoca's name means "Smoking Shield." The Spaniards sometimes spelled the king's name, Chimalpopocatzin.

Something ominous is struggling in the sky

During these last fortunate months,
curls of smoke, like hummingbirds,
flutter around Chimalpopoca's gorgeous head.

The successors of Quetzalcóatl tell us that our maize will not frost;
all the cacao and cotton that we have sown will come up well.

But tonight the high priests see something ominous
struggling in the sky.

Like thieves, they bury this knowledge.

So Chimalpopoca, our beautiful boy, our lord,
sees no omens swimming in the heavens.

Our king paints a poem of *moon against mountain,*
moonlight brushed on maguey branch,
        moon seasoning flame,
the dead passing through an arch of moonlight,
into soft wind. . .

This is his last poem.

Outside his shrine,
the assassins are gathering beneath a poisoned and bloated moon.

---

curls of smoke flutter, like hummingbirds, around Chimalpopoca's gorgeous head: Chimalpopoca (pronounced: Che-mal-po-po'-ca) reigned as Mexica king from 1417 to 1426. He was ten years old when he ascended to power. His name means "Smoking Shield" and it is glyphically represented in Mexica texts by a warrior's shield and curls of smoke. Chimalpopoca was the son of the previous ruler, Huitzilihutil. During Chimalpopoca's reign, Mexica power increased and the amount of tribute the Mexica paid to the Tepanecas was further reduced. The Mexica began to replace hut dwellings made with cane and reeds with structures made of stone. The Mexica constructed a wooden aqueduct to channel fresh water from mountain springs on the mainland to the island city. Mexica engineers and workers also built a stone causeway linking the Mexica island capital to the mainland city of Tlacopan. The causeway was equipped with a wooden drawbridge that could be raised to allow tall barges to navigate Lake Texcoco unobstructed. The bridge could also be completely removed to make the causeway impassable to invaders. An increase in Tenochtitlán's population created certain environmental problems, notably pollution in Lake Texcoco. **successors of Quetzalcóatl:** Mexica high priests were considered to be "divine of heart." They were regarded as successors of the revered creator god Quetzalcóatl. These high priests were called *quequetzalcoa,* which means "respected like lords." **maguey:** a cactus from which fiber was used as paper. **assassins are gathering beneath a poisoned moon:** Chimalpopoca was assassinated in 1426, at the age of nineteen. He was probably poisoned to death by the order of Maxtla, the Tepaneca king. Some accounts claim that a palace coup was engineered by the the royals Motecuhzoma Ilhuicamina, Tlacélel, and Itzcóatl, who succeeded Chimalpopoca to the Mexica throne. Some of the old chronicles suggest that the royal conspirators engaged the disaffected Tepanecas in the assassination. These accounts, however, are unsubstantiated.

If this is the last day of the world

It is said that Chimalpopoca will die at midnight.

Do the gods know this,
or are the killers tyrants of destiny?

The king and his priests stand speechless
as plumes of broad, black smoke churn from the mountain.

Ashen clouds race like mad beasts galloping in the sky,
and the prophets shake their heads in dismay.

Women stuff prayers into the ears of the gods
and the torches are lit inside the temples.

If this is the last day of the world,
the king will die with his hands folded like weeping herons.

Offerings of blue and black incense

The high priests enter the palace chamber
with pine torches flashing a hollow light
into a web of shadows.

An assassin, whose throat is covered with turquoise,
murmurs that the king is sleeping.

The holy men stagger before the body,
a carved, dead stone discarded against the silent wall of time.

The poison-bringer tells the priests to hurry,
so they quickly smear Chimalpopoca with the ointment of the dead,
burn offerings of blue and black incense,
and then flee into the night.

An assassin, whose throat is covered with turquoise, / murmurs that the king is sleeping: When King Huitzilíhuitl died in 1417, the royal council bypassed the dead king's brother, the valiant warrior Itzcóatl, electing instead Huitzilíhuitl's younger son, Chimalpopoca, who was also the favorite grandson of Tezozómoc, the powerful king of the Tepaneca empire. The Mexica ruling council, hoping to appease the Tepaneca, elected Chimalpopoca as the great speaker of the Mexica at the tender age of ten. The Mexica-Tepaneca détente did not last long. When Tezozómoc died, he was succeeded to the Tepaneca throne by his son, Maxtla, who publicly derided the Mexica. The new Tepaneca king reimposed on the Mexica the burdensome tributary obligations of earlier years. Chimalpopoca's inability to resist Maxtla's demands may have been a factor behind his assassination in 1426.

A sullen and brooding moon

We are always watched by a sullen and brooding moon.

But tonight, the stars are grieving perched high above us in their icy kingdom.

The poets scatter frozen flower petals and icicles
around the dead king, Chimalpopoca,
clothed in soft cotton and silence.

The king's eyes are pools of frozen water,
concealing the ancient mysteries of life and death.

The gods file past his body,
now only a feather tumbling in the wind.

---

only a feather tumbling in the wind: The sixteenth century historian and descendant of Texcocan royalty, Fernando de Alva Ixtilxóchitl, eulogized the dead king by writing: "Chimalpopoca was like a plume on your head that you have thrown away, like a necklace of precious stones that you have taken off."

The concubines scatter perfumed smoke inside the palace

13-Reed

Itzcóatl is poised, coiled like an angry snake
contemplating its prey.

The king sits menacingly with a bow and gilded arrows
on the ground, at his right hand.

His priests smear war paint, blood red, on his face,
crowning his head with green and gleaming plumes.

The concubines scatter perfumed smoke inside the palace
as the king chants before an idol of Huitzilopochtli,
enshrined in an ark of reeds.

The ambassadors and tax collectors bow their heads deeply,
as jewels and precious stones gleam from their wrists and throats.

They lay before the king bolts of green feathers,
bags of cochineal dye,
and bowls glittering in gold dust.

The lords of Coatepec and Xico place before him
many bins of maize and bins of beans.

Clear amber and bales of white cotton flourish at Itzcóatl's feet.

Outside the palace,
the clouds, shadows of the king, dance across the sky.

13-Reed: The Mexica year that corresponded to the Christian year 1427. **Itzcóatl:** Mexica king, 1427-1440. **an angry snake:** Itzcóatl's name means "Obsidian Serpent." **a bow and gilded arrows:** symbols of justice. **the king chants his reverence to Huitzilopochtli:** Itzcóatl's first act as king was to pay reverence to Huitzilopochtli, the god of war. The Spaniards sometimes spelled the king's name Itzcohuatzin or Itzcoatzin.

Tlacaélel's edict

The dead mock us continually.
They sit where they are, smug in what they know.
The dead are full of guile,
entrapping us in their incantations.

The dead rattle around in our heads
so that we speak only of them.

It is time for the bewitchment to be broken,
as one would break stone.

We must purge the past from the minds of the people,
shape their memories
according to our own will and contemplation.

It is not difficult to reimagine the pieces of the past.

So let history be what we want it to be:
idyllic, clotted with war,
triumphant.

As the Sun climbs towards its throne,
take the historians to the temple,
and kill them there.

Tlacaélel: (pronounced: Tla-kah-EL-el) (1397-1487) the younger brother of Motecuhzoma Ilhuicamina and nephew of Itzcóatl. Tlacaélel never reigned as king, but he exerted a major influence on Mexica society as a military commander, diplomat, and imperial strategist. Tlacaélel first came to prominence as a general in the Mexica army during
the reign of King Itzcóatl. Under King Motecuhzoma Ilhuicamina, Tlacaélel held the title
of *Cihuacóatl* (pronounced: Chee-wha-coh'-atl), meaning literally "Woman Snake." In
that position, Tlacaélel ruled as a prime minister and high priest. Under Tlacaélel's influence, the worship of the war god and lord of the sun, Huitzilopochtli (pronounced:
Weet-zeel-oh-póhsh-tlee) was elevated from a relatively minor deity to an imperial cult
that was predicated on the newly-manufactured belief that the war god demanded a con-
stant supply of human hearts so that he would keep the sun blazing in the sky. The Mex-

ica prosecuted wars against surrounding city-states in large measure to procure captives to be sacrificed to placate the tutelary god Huitzilopochtli. The privilege and power of the Mexica monarchy intensified under Tlacaélel and the Mexica kingdom itself was enlarged into an empire. Tlacaélel developed a mystical and militant vision of Mexica society as the chosen nation of the Sun. The cultish devotion to the ferocious god Huitzilopochtli drove home the idea that the war god and the Mexica state were omnipotent and that both must be rigorously obeyed. Tlacaélel served as *Cihuacóatl* under four Mexica kings: Motecuhzoma Ilhuicamina, Axayácatl, Tizoc, and Ahuítzotl. **We must purge the past from the minds of the people, shape their memories according to our contemplation and will:** Tlacaélel was hypersensitive to the subservient status that the Mexica had endured during their early history. In 1431 (the Mexica year 4-Reed), he persuaded Mexica King Itzcóatl to destroy the sacred texts which included historical accounts, largely written by other peoples, and which were mostly unfavorable to the Mexica. The chronicles recorded how the Mexica were mere tributaries of the established, more powerful city-states in the central valley of Mexico and how the Mexica had suffered numerous military defeats in the past. Either Tlacaélel or King Itzcóatl declared: "It is not fitting that our people should know these pictures. Our people, our subjects, will be lost and our land destroyed, for these pictures are full of lies." Charles C. Mann has described the destruction of the codices as "Orwellian." In his novel *1984,* George Orwell wrote: "Who controls the past, controls the future." Eager to command the future, Tlacaélel ordered new historical chronicles composed that emphasized Mexica greatness (with ties to the Toltecas and Teotihuacán) and Huitzilopochtli's preeminence. Please see the poem "From flower and song." The revisionist history portrayed the Mexica as the chosen people of Huitzilopochtli, the children of the Eagle and the Sun, and direct descendants of the distinguished Toltecas, through Culhuacán. Meanwhile, the refurbished Mexica theology elevated Huitzilopochtli, the Mexica sun god and war god, to the same exalted plateau, and to an even higher plateau, of the great Tolteca gods Quetzalcóatl and Tezcatlipoca. **the temple:** the temple of the war god Huitzilopochtli, in the Tenochtitlán, the Mexica capital. **As the sun climbs towards its throne:** an allusion to the rising sun, a representation of the power of Huitzilopochtli, the ambassador to the sun. According to the overhauled Mexica theology, Huitzilopochtli had held out a promise to the Mexica if they obeyed only him and became warriors: The great god had said to Mexica high priests as they searched for a new homeland after leaving Aztlán: "I shall make you lords and kings of whatever there is in the world, wherever it may be, and you will have innumerable and endless vassals that will pay you tribute. . . You will be limited by nothing. . .whatever your greeds are, you will be satisfied; you will take women where and when you please. . .you will receive gifts of everything—the best food, the greatest ease, fragrance, flowers, tobacco, song, everything. . . And you will see all this, for this is my true task and I was sent here for this. . ." In another version, Huitzilopochtli ordered the Mexica to search for "The cactus where the eagle stands, where the eagle eats and is sunning itself. There we will be, there we will show our might, there we will wait. There we will meet different peoples who will be our vassals. With our bows and arrows we will fight those who surround us. We will conquer all of them, we will take them prisoner. There we will raise our city, Tenochtitlán, the place where the eagle screams, the place where fishes swim, Tenochtitlán! Great things will come to pass there!"

From flower and song

Itzcóatl, emblazoned in turquoise and quetzal feathers,
gathers the sacred manuscripts before him.

These books tell what has been and what will be.
They mark each detail of a mad and willful humanity.

There is a tremendous pull from the other world.

All the ancestral spirits have struggled back from the dead.
They crowd around Itzcóatl to offer him their heavy, sullen hearts.

The great speaker shuts his eyes,
yet ghosts still hover over obscure squares of flame
smoldering in the darkest days,
in days singed dark by a cursed and haggard luck.

How shall this lamentable past be purged from each mind and heart?

How shall our chronicles be cleansed?

Itzcóatl casts each defeat, each infamy, into pits seething with succulent fire.
History is consumed by stormy smoke.

What was once, will no longer be known.

Itzcóatl tells the poets and soothsayers to make a new past
from incense and copal smoke,
from flower and song.

But still the fates loom darkly.

In the days to come,

men, with faces made of chalk,
will rise from the sea,
eager to unsheathe lightning that incinerates trees and crumbles mountains.

Then the sun will become wind, blowing away.

And each one of Itzcóatl's descendants shall harden like wood,
petrified wood.

Itzcóatl: Mexica ruler (known as the huei tlatoani pronounced: ooeh tlah-toh-ah-ni) or, revered speaker. Itzcóatl (pronounced: Eets-koh-AT-tl) reigned from 1427 to 1440. His name means "Obsidian Serpent." Itzcóatl was the son of Acamapichtli, brother of Huitzilíhuitl, and uncle of Chimalpopoca. In 1431, Itzcóatl ordered the pictographic manuscripts (which the Spaniards later called codices) destroyed. The sacred books were horizontal panels comprised of pages of deerskin or bark paper stitched together and that folded and unfolded like an accordion. These manuscripts contained Mexica religious beliefs, iconography, history, calendars, auguries, and outlines of rituals and customs. Itzcóatl decreed that the books were to be destroyed and a new chronicle of the past and a new cosmology invented. Eloise Quiñoes Keber argues that modern day criteria for historical accuracy cannot be applied to Mexica (or, Aztec) versions of history. "What is important," she asserts, "is that [Mexica historical accounts tell] us how the Aztecs viewed themselves. . .[Mexica chronicles allow] us to see how the Aztecs officially presented their world to themselves as well as to others. Even if they blatantly reshaped their past, it was a vision of themselves that helped to structure their present and their future." Nevertheless, Quiñoes Keber suggests that Itzcóatl's burning of the old texts "might be seen in light of twentieth century examples of revisionist history as well as recent trends in historiography that view history as an ideological construct, as much interpretation as 'facts.'" For additional information, please see the poem "Tlacaélel's edict." **mad and willful humanity:** this phrase was coined by Paul Bourget in 1893. **flower and song:** the Mexica pictograph for poetry was a compound glyph (or, pictograph or ideograph) combining the concepts of flower and song. **In the days to come:** a reference to the arrival of Hernán Cortés and the Spanish conquistadores in 1519. **men, with faces made of chalk:** the Mexica saw the Spaniards as men with faces that resembled white chalk. **eager to unsheathe lightning:** Mexica scribes recorded that Spanish cannons discharged lightning that splintered mountains and blew away trees.

Huitzilopochtli, in the beginning and in the end

Huitzilopochtli sits in the dark clouds,
cross-legged,
dressed richly in resplendent feathers.
Before him glimmer a golden bow and arrow
and a brazier full of human hearts still warm.

He sits, magnificent and unperturbed,
frozen, a bronze effigy,
a carving in stone, motionless.

Still he sends tremors in the earth,
and tramples the enemy moon and stars.

The clouds disperse before clear skies. . .

Huitzilopochtli raises his fire serpent to the sun.

His destiny burns a broad, black trail of smoke
across the mighty heavens.

All his prophecies are seared by the sun's fire,
engraved in stone by religious light.

His words are seeds that flower violently in our hearts.

Huitzilopochtli intoxicates us with war.
He emboldens us: *Be strong. Do not rest.*
You are the Mexica, my chosen ones!

Look at our enemies gathered in their war array,

wearing paper crowns and nettles.

How arrogantly they wave their banners from side to side
and shake their rattlebells!

My Mexica, shoot your arrows angrily!

Fall on these adversaries, finish them off,
trample them like grass.

Who will mourn them?
Who will remember them?

It is only you, the Mexica kings, who rule the earth
in my name's sake.

Huitzilopochtli is our beginning and our end.
We give prayers and offerings only to him.
We eat effigies of our fiery lord from corn paste and seeds.
This is our communion with divinity.

Our hummingbird wizard is here and there,
furiously
         slashing
across the sky,
like time.

And when he is not here, still he is here:
for our lord watches us in his obsidian mirror.

We on the earth move in that glass, stuck in that prism,
blessed but forlorn,
like so many ghosts burned into the face of ice.

Huitzilopochtli gives us health and harvest,
but he leaves us wondering,
always grasping at straws: Why are we like flowers
that bloom only for a little while here?

Huitzilopochtli: According to Mexica religion, the Mexica were commanded to move south from their Aztlán homeland by Huitzilopochtli (pronounced: Weet-zeel-oh-póhsh-tlee), their most revered and feared god. The name Huitzilopochtli means "Humming-bird Wizard." He was the fiery lord of the sun and the god of war. Huitzilopochtli wore a helmet shaped like a hummingbird head while donning hummingbird feathers on his left leg. The hummingbird was seen as a symbol of resurrection as the Mexica believed that the bird died during the dry season and was reborn as the rainy season began. Huitzilopochtli brandished the fire serpent, the *xiuhcóatl* (pronounced: Shee-ooh-kwa-tl), a divine weapon that perpetually guaranteed the triumph of the Mexica armies. In some accounts, the *xiuhcóatl* was represented as a ray of sun, the destroyer of night. In addition to his fire serpent, Huitzilopochtli held a mirror of obsidian (or, volcanic) glass into which he gazed to see the actions of mortals.

The Mexica were inspired to move south by a specific religious vision that was conveyed to them by Huitzilopochtli himself. This prophecy told them to search for a home where they found an eagle with a serpent in its beak perched on a tall cactus. Huitzilopochtli ordered the Mexica to search for "the cactus where the eagle stands, where the eagle eats and is sunning itself. There we will be, there we will show our might, there we will wait. There we will meet different peoples who will be our vassals. With our bows and arrows we will fight those who surround us. We will conquer all of them, we will take them prisoner. There we will raise our city, Tenochtitlán, the place where the eagle screams, the place where fishes swim. Tenochtitlán! Great things will come to pass there!" In addition, according to Mexica sacred books, Huitzilopochtli had held out a promise to the Mexica *if* they obeyed only him and became warriors: The great god said: "I shall make you lords and kings of whatever there is in the world, wherever it may be, and you will have innumerable and endless vassals that will pay you tribute. . . You will be limited by nothing. . .whatever your greeds are, you will be satisfied; you will take women where and when you please. . .you will receive gifts of everything—the best food, the greatest ease, fragrance, flowers, tobacco, song, every-thing. . . And you will see all this, for this is my true task and I was sent here for this." During their search for Huitzilopchtli's promised land, the Mexica came to see them-selves as a messianic people—the chosen people of the gods. They had visions of grandeur and imperial power. When the Mexica wandered south, they carried with them effigies of Huitzilopochtli. These images, carried aloft, were to protect the Mexica migrants from misfortune.

Around 1325 (the Mexica year 2-House)—after a long migration—that included a period they spent in servitude—the Mexica encountered the sign that signaled the end of their wandering. The Mexica saw the nopal cactus growing from a rock and perched on top of it was the predicted eagle, with its wings extended toward the rays of the sun. In the eagle's claw was a very elegant serpent. That breathtaking sign was discovered on a rattlesnake-infested, swampy island in the middle of the shallow, saline Lake Texcoco (pronounced: Tesh-koh-koh), which was later drained to build Mexico City. The island was so desolate and unappealing that it had never been permanently occupied. The Mexica named their new home Tenochtitlán, which means "Place Next to the Prickly Pear Cactus." The eagle and the serpent and the cactus became Mexica icons and later symbols of the modern Mexican state. Because of Huitzilopochtli's identification with the sun, King Itzcóatl and his chief minister Tlacélel apotheosized the deity as "the Giver and Preserver of Life." **tramples the enemy moon and stars:** Huitzilopochtli, the lord of the sun, despised the moon and stars. **His words are seeds that flower violently in our hearts:** In addition to guiding the Mexica to their new home, Huitzilopochtli was also the belligerent inspiration of Mexica wars and territorial expansion. Huitzilopochtli represented the militaristic, imperial Mexica spirit. Each day, Huitzilopochtli escorted the sun to its zenith. As payment for these heroic acts, Huitzilopochtli demanded human hearts and blood for his food and drink. **We eat effigies of our fiery lord from corn paste and seeds:** During festivals held during times of war, the Mexica demonstrated their adoration to Huitzilopochtli by constructing an image of their ferocious god of war from molded maize paste, amaranth seeds, and honey. The representation of Huitzilopochtli was then "killed" by a Mexica soldier who shot an arrow with a flinthead into its vegetable heart. The heart was presented to the Mexica king while his elite warriors ate fragments of the venerated effigy. Those who consumed the "flesh" of Huitzilopochtli entered into a yearlong period of penance and religious obligation. **We are like flowers that bloom only for a little while:** The Mexica believed that their power was not timeless; they understood that their downfall was inevitable. A Mexica poet wrote: "We live for the day. Our lives are like flowers. The earth is ours in name only."

Itzcóatl chastens the dissidents

The Mexica priests work in solitude inside the temples,
sprinkling fine gold dust on faded scriptures
and nodding cautiously at spirits dancing in puffs of smoke.

They watch the stars, to ascertain their course,
to know their signs and influences.

They track the heavenly apparitions that lean across the sky.

The Tenochca speak of history in symbols and mists.

They raise effigies of the dead
as if they were the envoys from the netherworld.

Their king, Itzcóatl, rails at the enemies
of his kingdom.

He chastens the dissidents,
bewitching them with the cryptic aura of his religion.

Itzcóatl, chastens the dissidents / and sacrifices the enemies of his kingdom:
When he came to power in 1427, Itzcóatl was forty-six or forty-seven years old and had
long been established as a distinguished warrior. Soon after his coronation, Itzcóatl addressed his warriors, predicting, "You will make many peoples tremble." The Warlord-
King Itzcóatl believed that it was his mission "to gather together all the nations" in the
service of Huitzilopochtli. A year after Itzcóatl's ascension, the Tepanecas, the long-
standing rivals of the Mexica, worried as the distinguished warrior Itzcóatl was elected
king of the Mexica, and were alarmed by indications that the Mexica would launch a
program of military and territorial aggrandizement. The Tepanecas blockaded the Mexica capital, stationing guards on the approaches to the city. Some of Itzcóatl's ministers
advised sending an embassy to the Tepanecas, so that an effigy of the war god
Huitzilopochtli could be delivered into the hands of Tepaneca rulers as a sign of Mexica submission. Itzcóatl and Tlacaélel refused to appease their adversaries and instead
retaliated with a major military campaign against the Tepancas, which included a siege
of Azcapotzalco, the Tepaneca capital. After an epic 114-day battle, the Mexica overran
the city in 1428 and the Tepaneca king, Maxtla, was slain and many of his subjects fled

into the mountains. Some scholars have argued that the Tepaneca empire was already disintegrating at the time of Itzcóatl's triumph. But even if Tepaneca power was in decline in 1428, the Mexica victory at Azcapitzalco marked the end of Tepaneca hegemony in the Valley of Mexico and the beginning of Mexica imperial power. In defeat, Tepancea rulers pledged lands, labor, and tribute goods to the Mexica. **Tenochca:** the Mexica citizens of Tenochtitlán.

Graven images

I am the will of Tezcatlipoca,
embodied in this flesh and blood.

I glean what I glean from our lord,
who moves like a wind at night.

My face burns with an ancient fury unbound
from the first fires.

With this heat,
sear the image of the Obsidian Serpent on sky and stone;
cauterize it on your hearts.

Graven images: Itzcóatl (r.1427-1440) was the first Mexica king to order his image engraved on stone. **the will of Tezcatlipoca:** god of the night sky and material things. He was also the patron deity of the Mexica royal house. Mexica kings were seen as Tezcatlipoca's representatives on earth. Please see the poem "Lord of the smoking mirror." **from our lord:** Tezcatlipoca. **the image of the Obsidian Serpent:** Itzcóatl name means "Obsidian Serpent." Following Itzcóatl's death in 1440, a Mexica minister announced: "He cannot return. No one will see him here among those that are living, or those that will be born." The *cihuacóatl,* or prime minister, Tlacaélel added his own lofty oratory when he addressed the Mexica army: "Now the light that illuminated you is extinguished, the voice at whose sound all the kingdom moved is stilled, and the mirror in which all men saw themselves is darkened. Thus, illustrious warriors, it is not fitting that the kingdom be left in obscurity; may another sun rise to give it light. . . Who does it seem to you to be best fitted to follow in the footsteps of our dead king? Who will preserve for us what he has won?" Motecuhzoma Ilhuicamina, a nephew of the late Itzcóatl, was elected king of the Mexica.

The Angry Lord Shoots His Arrows Into the Sky

Our lord, Motecuhzoma Chalchiuhtlatonac,
was born as the sun heaved its flames in every direction across the sky.

Our king is that sun burning through the clouds.

He who is sanctified and severe,
strikes against evil,
bringing health and harvest to his kingdom.

His temperament is the temper of the gods,
who protect and menace men,
charming and chiding them until death carries them away.

Our lord turns his head from the intoxicating flavors
and sends away the concubines pasted only in feathers.

His laws give off sparks of divine fire
so that society is ordered and orderly,
where all might live in their place.

He has made the waters come glistening into the city.

He separates the fresh water from the waters glimmering with salt.

He dredges light from the dusk
and burnishes violence with blossoming starlight.

Motecuhzoma's armies reach the end of the world,
where the land falls away into the sea,

where aliens crane their ugly heads like ragged, unkempt flowers.

Mexica soldiers move among these strangers who speak in harsh and raucous tongues.
These foreigners stagger in fog or smoke
because the gods have thrown shadows on their eyes.

These aliens abide always in ripened darkness.

Let their idols disintegrate
as their arrogant language tumbles into the deepest silence.

Cemanahuac Tenochca Tlapan.

The Angry Lord Shoots His Arrow Into the Sky: Mexica King Motecuhzoma Il-huicamina (pronounced: Maw-tay-kwah-SOH-mah Eel-eeh-kah-mee-nah) reigned from 1440-1469. His name means "Angry Lord Who Shoots His Arrows Into the Sky." The name derives from *tecuh (tli), (mo)çuma,* meaning, to frown from anger. *Ilhuica (tl),* sky; *mina,* to shoot an arrow. Later, he would be given yet another name, Chalchiuhtla-tonac—which means "He Who Shines Like Jade." Among the Spanish variations on the spelling of the king's name is Moteucçoma. Motecuhzoma Ilhuicamina was a son of Huitzilíhuitl and a nephew of Itzcóatl. Before ascending to power, he had earned a reputation as a valiant warrior and an experienced diplomat. The Mexica often fused folklore with history, including the "historical" account of the miraculous conception of Motecuhzoma Ilhuicamina. The Spaniards sometimes spelled the king's name, Moteuc-zomatzin Ilhuicaminatzin. **Motecuhzoma Chalchiuhtlatonac, / was born as the sun heaved its flames in every direction across the sky:** Motecuhzoma Ilhuicamina was said to have been born at dawn, as the sun appeared over the horizon. **He who is sanctified and severe, / strikes against evil:** Motecuhzoma was described in the *Codex Mendoza* as "very serious, severe, and virtuous. . .of good temper and judgment and an enemy of evil." Although the king enjoyed talking to common men who constructed the city's infrastructure, his subjects gravely feared to gaze at him when he appeared in public. Motecuhzoma, whose name can also mean "the Offended One," could be cruel, severe, and forbidding. **Our lord turns his head from the intoxicating flavors:** In spite of the great wealth and privileges that he commanded as king of the Mexica, Motecuhzoma Ilhuicamina led an austere life, exercising moderation in consuming the intoxicating *pulque* drink and in womanizing. **His laws give off sparks of divine fire:** Motecuhzoma Ilhuicamina's government enforced rigid sumptuary laws regulating strict morality in public behavior. These laws were called "sparks of divine fire" because they were considered to be inspired by the gods. The laws also enforced a rigid social stratification between the nobility, commoners, and slaves so that "all might live within their station." These laws prescribed a clear division of conduct for nobles and commoners. Only members of the nobility were permitted to wear cotton clothing. Under penalty of death, commoners were prohibited from wearing cotton and could only dress in garments made of maguey fiber. Only nobles and decorated warriors could live in two-story houses. Only great lords were permitted to adorn themselves in gold lip, ear, or nose plugs or wear jewelry made with precious stones. The new laws also prohibited the king from appearing publicly, except in times of emergency. The state was required to establish schools in the commoners' districts where boys would learn theology, warfare, and proper social behavior. Motecuhzoma's government created a quasi-noble status, called *quauhpilli,* or eagle lords, a near-noble status awarded to commoners who distinguished themselves in battle. **He has made the waters come glistening into the city:** Motecuhzoma ordered a new aqueduct, built with stones and sod, constructed from the springs of Chapultepec hill to Tenochtitlán. The waters of Chapultepec were considered to have regenerative qualities, purging sin and physical sickness. The aqueduct boasted two channels so that one could carry clean water into the island city when the other channel was being cleaned or repaired. In addition, Motecuhzoma Ilhuicamina ordered the hill of Chapultepec (meaning "Hill of the Grasshopper") beautified, namely by planting *ahuehuetes* (or, cypress trees). The king declared Chapultepec hill a place of refuge for Mexica royals, and he ordered his likeness carved into the hillside. **He separates the fresh water from the waters glistening with salt:** The Mexica capital was always vulnerable to flooding in heavy rains and rising water levels in Lake Texcoco. Hoping to at least contain the threat of flooding, Motecuhzoma Ilhuicamina ordered the construction of a dike to bifurcate the lake. Constructed of heavy logs and rocks, the hydraulic structure was more than nine miles wide and thirty-three feet wide. The dike boasted two parallel walls of logs with the area between them filled with 300,000 cubic meters of rocks and sod. In addition to stemming floodwaters, the dike also controlled the salinity of the lake water by separating the salt water from the waters of the contiguous Lakes Xochimilco and Chalco, which received streams of fresh water from snow-crowned volcanoes. **Motecuhzoma's armies reach the end of the world:** During Motecuhzoma Ilhuicamina's reign, Mexica military conquests reached as far as Oaxaca and the Gulf of Mexico. The Mexica received tribute payments of tropical feathers, precious stones, as well as gold, silver, and copper from the regions the Mexica subordinated. **aliens crane their ugly heads like ragged, unkempt flowers:** those people whom the Mexica defeated. **Cemanahuac Tenochca Tlapan:** Náhuatl, The Land Surrounded by Water is Tenochca Territory. The Mexica citizens of Tenochtitlán, the Mexica capital, also called themselves the Tenochca, the inhabitants of Tenochtitlán. The phrase Cemanahuac Tenochca Tlapan was a resounding expression of Mexica nationalism.

The magicians and wizards leave
the temples at dawn

The magicians and wizards leave the temples at dawn.
They scatter in dim light
carrying sparkling gifts and effigies of the king.

These ambassadors move haltingly through time,
meandering across the kingdoms of memory.

They are clairvoyant and somber men searching in the dark light for Aztlán,
the Place of White-Feathered Herons,
the birthplace of the Mexica ancestors.

Where is Aztlán, where our god Huitzilopochtli first touched the earth?

Where is the happy land of ducks and swans swimming in marshes?
Birds whistled and sang there in the shade of trees.
All was blessed; even silence was musical, in the dim past, in Aztlán.

But winter came to that place after our ancestors left it.
Then there was nothing left there but thorns
and pointed rocks, prickly plants
and trees with spines.

So now the Tenochca envoys search barren land for traces, touchstones, and roots
leading back to the dawn of our people.

Is it possible that they will find Coatlicue,
dressed in her skirt of writhing snakes,
she who gave birth to the god of war,
the ambassador to the sun?

The magicians use charms and smoking light, they cajole incantations,
to turn themselves into birds, swept by wind and blown back to Aztlán.

When the wind dies, Coatlicue appears before the travelers,

who once again assume the shapes of men.
They present the ancient mother of the warrior god
excited words of Mexica triumphs
and the names of each king since Acamapichtli.
They place smoky quartz, bowls of gold dust, and cacao at her feet.

But the goddess rebuffs them and their trail of offerings:

"Why do you hold high your heads smugly
when in fact your heads should be lowered in shame?

"I do not care for these gifts,
for they are only tokens of your conceit.

"If you could look ahead, into distant days,
you would know that your kingdom, and everything in it, will be smoke
blowing away in a strong wind."

The magicians and wizards leave the temples at dawn: According to Mexica historical accounts, which were often interwoven with folklore, in about 1450, Motecuhzoma Ilhuicamina sent perhaps as many as sixty magicians to locate Aztlán, the ancestral homeland of the Mexica nation. The king hoped that the Mexica who still lived in Aztlán could hear about, and share in, the spectacular military and material accomplishments of the Mexica empire. The wizards were supplied with magnificent gifts of cotton mantles, precious stones, and resplendent feathers to bestow on the residents of Aztlán. After an arduous trek across a desert wilderness, Motecuhzoma's envoys reached the purported birthplace of the war god and ambassador to the sun, Huitzilopochtli. These messengers encountered a demon that metamorphosed them into birds. Having been transformed, the envoys flew to a distant location where, having returned to human form, they met fellow Mexica speaking the Náhuatl language. However, rather than being bedazzled by the rise of Tenochtitlán, the kinsmen at Aztlán berated Motecuhzoma's ambassadors for their luxurious and decadent ways that were so far removed from the hard, demanding life ways in Aztlán. Still in the ancestral homeland, the magicians were granted an audience with the goddess Coatlicue, the ancient mother of the warlord Huitzilopochtli. The wizards presented the goddess with the array of sumptuous offerings, which she cast aside. Disinterested in accounts of Mexica triumphs, Coatlicue forecast doom, prophesizing that the Mexica empire would be toppled.

The goddess Coatlicue had a ghastly appearance: her lower mouth was a fleshless jawbone; her hair was long and ragged; and she had two flint knives of sacrifice attached to her forehead. Her name means, "She of the Skirt of Snakes" because she always wore a dress of writhing serpents. Her hands and feet were tipped with monstrous claws for devouring sacrificial human victims. From that human prey, Coatlicue wore a necklace fashioned from human hearts and lacerated hands. Her face was painted in chalky white. According to Mexica theology, the goddess appeared before mortals "covered with chalk, like a court lady. She wore ear-plugs, obsidian ear-plugs. She appeared in white, garbed in white, standing white, pure white."

The buzzards are gathering, thickly, in the sky

Who does not know that these are years, like calamities,
growing among us like weeds?

See how the locusts descend from thin air
to eat what was grown for Huitzilopochtli's children.
The earth itself is famished.
Our jaguars are staggering. They are dying,
one after another.

The waters climb in the ninth year of the king's reign;
the waters thicken and tumble without regard to life or handiwork.

And then the frosts come, before they are due.
And the crops crumble in the cold.
And the people starve by the withered corn.

So there is anguish from here to there.

The prognosticators say that these are locusts, then floods, followed by hunger
visited upon the people by provoked gods.
The earth is rebelling against man.
How shall the capricious and mercurial lords be placated?
What would placate them? Or what do the gods want?

The priests consult patterns of clouds and the texture of smoke
to learn the prophecies which are carried on the wind,
to see the visions, the auguries that plague this land.

The religious men have studied our legacy,
the record of who we are
and who we once were.

They tell us the things we cherish are tokens that mean nothing
in our last and dying days.

These wise men tell us that the buzzards are gathering, thickly, in the sky,
swirling, swirling until they become dense smoke.

Who does not know that these are years, like calamities: The Mexica celebrated sweeping military success and economic prosperity during the reign of Motecuhzoma Ilhuicamina (pronounced: Maw-tay-kwah-SOH-mah Eel-eeh-kah-mee-nah). Sometimes his name is pronounced, "Mohk-the-ZOO-mah." However, those years were also marred by a series of natural catastrophes: a plague of locusts in 1446 and severe flooding in the Mexica capital in 1449. A four-year drought, started by early frosts in 1450, led to widespread famine. **The earth is rebelling against man:** The Mexica described the famine as "the earth rebelling against man." **Then how shall the capricious and mercurial lords be placated?:** In an effort to appease the gods, the Mexica government ordered the numbers of human sacrifices increased. Beginning in 1450, the Mexica launched the "flowery wars" against neighboring city-states, especially Tlaxcala. A war of flowers *(xochiyaoyotl)* provided Mexica warriors with combat training and testing and the opportunity to capture prisoners of war to be sacrificed to placate the deities. For the Mexica military theocracy, a prolonged peace was dangerous as it deprived the gods of their steady diet of human hearts and blood. If the gods were not placated, the entire world would be decimated. The wars of flowers intensified contempt for the Mexica. The Náhuatl word for sacrifice, *nextlaoaliztli,* meant an "act of payment." **Huitzilopochtli's children:** The Mexica regarded themselves as children of Huitzilopochtli, the lord of the sun and the god of war.

The last decree of Hue Hue Motecuhzoma

After this decree, there is no other:

When I am at last still,
cut out my heart,
and place it, gently, among the reeds.

Let the eagle and snake devour
the vessel of my passions
so that the fire and ice shall bleed
into the memories of my people.

Hue Hue Motecuhzoma: Hue Hue indicates "the elder." This phrase is used to distinguish Motecuhzoma (I) Ilhuicamina, from his great-grandson, Motecuhzoma (II) Xocoyotzin, who ruled the Mexica from 1502-1520. **After this decree, there is no other:** After a momentous reign of nineteen years, Motecuhzoma Ilhuicamina died in 1469. **eagle and snake:** were revered in Mexica culture.

Hue Hue Motecuhzoma is dead

If I could have my life again,
I would be a poet, not a king.

Only the hearts of poets live eternally
in flower and song.

The weeping servants fan the face of the dying king,
who breathes fitfully, like an aged jaguar.

The light escapes from his eyes
and his breathing grows shallow.

The body tightens and trembles,
as the earth quakes in days of restlessness.

Motecuhzoma closes his eyes finally,
two stones silently blind.

The night birds swoon in the air
and the world darkens.

The dead king is bathed in water sweetened
with fragrant flowers.

The poets and priests and envoys from distant places pray
as the king's knees are brought to the chest, bound in pale grave clothes.

The incense of copal swirls slowly, dancing mournfully
with the spirits of the dead.

The honored body burns on a fire of pitch pine,
the smoke rising like tall, dark cranes taking the sky.

Hue Hue Motecuhzoma: Motecuhzoma Ilhuicamina, Mexica king, 1440-1469. **I would be a poet, not a king:** The Mexica depicted the word "poetry" using the glyphs for flower and song—gifts of the gods. Poets were believed to possess a "deified heart." Motecuhzoma Ilhuicamina did not want his sons to become rulers; instead, he hoped that they would be artisans and craftsmen. Motecuhzoma was succeeded to the Mexica throne by his grandson, Axayácatl. **The honored body burns on a fire of pitch pine:** the bodies of dead Mexica kings were cremated.

The oldest gods polish our dreams in gleaming turquoise

We Mexica kings were born in the interior of wind.
    We know the mysteries of prayer and rain.
Our meditations and edicts whirl and whine
in both starry and starless nights.

The oldest gods polish our dreams in gleaming turquoise,
in the smoke of copal incense.
Their words to us are shiny gems,
worshiped like ghosts holding clouds.

The last fires flower from the remains of our dead poets;
tears and smoke mingle at sunset.

I, Axayácatl, the reigning king of the Mexica, know what I know.
I know what has been said inside the temples.
I have seen the artists binding age to age,
painting wisdom in illuminated manuscripts that radiate like the eyes of the gods.
I have run my fingers across these beautiful books painted in black and red,
painted with darkness and painted with light.

Like my grandfather, Motecuhzoma Chalchiuhtlatonac,
I glimpsed what was and what will never be again.
The *tlamatinimes* held the mirror of memory to my eyes.
So I studied the light and shade through the clouds,
and I saw the faces of the dead staring at me
    with their eyes gleaming with precious stones.
The dead are the guardians of wisdom, jealously keeping in their hearts
the undecipherable signs, like the clouds that pass over us,
then are gone forever.

But my eyes can see far beyond,

for I have touched the prophecies painted on deerskin and maguey fiber.

I can see farther into the stone.

I know many things.

I know of things that I cannot tell you.

Axayácatl: (pronounced: Ah-sha-ya-ka'-tl) the grandson of Motecuhzoma Ilhuicamina, ruled the Mexica from 1469-1481. In addition to his martial abilities, Axayácatl was an accomplished poet. ***tlamatinimes:*** wise men.

The dark lament of Axayácatl

Let us hang ourselves to the rays of the sun
so that we may drip fire,
drop by drop,
upon the earth,
the place of our tribulation.

Why should we not wish that this abode
be reduced to glowing and scattered embers?

For the once florid dreams of war have turned barren,
colorless, without pleasure,
a realm of dreams turned to waste.

Even our jade is shattered,
and our calendars tell us nothing.

The braziers which were once full of hearts
are no longer full.
Our own hearts, once joyous,
now sink heavily,
buried in sky waters of mud.

The gods are staggered in their distress:

They send heavy clouds sprawling from this place
to the very edge of the unknown world.

Grotesque birds squawk obnoxiously
as if the sky is all theirs.

Why are these dumb birds happier than we?

What can our priests and elders tell us about the days to follow?

Will the wizards say which fears we should ignore
and which should freeze us in paralysis?

Axayácatl: (pronounced: Ah-sha-ya-ka'-tl) the grandson of Motecuhzoma Ilhuicamina, ruled the Mexica from 1469-1481. His name means "Face of Water." Axayácatl was about nineteen years old when he ascended to the Mexica throne. The *Codex Mendoza* depicts Axayácatl as proud, restless, and deeply feared by his subjects. He was elected *huei tlatoani* (or, great speaker) in large measure because of his valor in war. As king, Axayácatl sought to add to his reputation as a warrior. During his coronation war, he led Mexica soldiers, for the first time, to the Pacific coast. The Spaniards sometimes spelled the king's name, Axayácatzin. **For the once florid dreams of war have turned barren:** Axayácatl was preoccupied with military conquests and demonstrated little interest in domestic affairs. Early in his reign, a civil war among the Mexica erupted between Tenochtitlán and its neighboring sister city, Tlateloco, which was the site of a major market and home to many Tenochca merchants. The fighting was precipitated by young Mexica men who had raped Tlateloca women and the maltreatment of Axayácatl's sister, who was married to Moquihuix, lord of Tlateloco. In 1473, Axayácatl dispatched messengers to Tlateloco to present its leaders with ritual feathers, an obsidian-toothed club, and shield, symbols of impending war. Led by Axayácatl, the Mexica army crushed Tlateloco in a lightning attack. Tlateloco's independence was ended and the city was annexed to Tenochtitlán. The Tlatelolca subsequently proclaimed themselves to be merchants who would provide tribute to Tenochtitlán. The following year, Axayácatl led his troops to the northwest to take the Valley of Toluca. Axayácatl was seriously, although not fatally, wounded in the campaign against the Tolucans. Having returned to his capital, the Mexica king anointed a grandiose statue of Huitzilopochtli with blood from his wounded leg as an offering of thanksgiving for his delivery from battle. The thanksgiving was short-lived as the Mexica soon suffered a crushing defeat to the Tarascan empire. The 1478 war against the Tarascans began fortuitously for the Mexica. Led by the king, Axayácatl, the Mexica army surrounded and captured the Tarascan city of

Xiquipilco, following brutal hand-to-hand fighting. But after that initial success, the war turned disastrous for Mexica forces. Driving deeper into Tarascan territory, the Mexica army of 24,000 confronted a vast Tarascan force of 40,000 warriors. The Mexica were not only outnumbered, but they also had to contend against the superior metal armaments of their Tarascan adversaries. The Tarascans were superior metallurgists; their copper arrowheads, darts, and spears killed Mexica warriors in large numbers, "like flies which fell into the water." The Mexica were slaughtered on the home ground of the Tarascans. After a two-day bloodletting, the Mexica were driven into full retreat to Tenochtitlán, where they were met with weeping and mourning. The defeat, which left Axayácatl in deep despair, was the worst in Mexica history and the first indication of imperial Mexica vulnerability. Vassal subjects in towns and provinces across the Mexica empire were emboldened by the news of the Mexica defeat. The Tarascans benefited from secure communication and supply lines and knowledge of their home terrain. Yet in spite of their stunning triumph, the Tarascans did not press any subsequent campaign against the Mexica, mainly because Tenochtitlán could not be easily attacked from Tarascan territory. Thus, the Mexica were able to contain the defeat to the Tarascans to a single, terrible episode. The Mexica never launched a significant campaign to reverse the defeat to the Tarascans, but Axayácatl attempted, instead, to restore the image of the Mexica empire, as well as rehabilitate his own image, by prosecuting a "war of flowers" against Tliliuhquitepec, an independent city-state in the Puebla-Tlaxcala Valley. He also suppressed rebellions that had broken out in Ocuilan, Huexotla, and Xiquipilco. **sky waters:** the sea; also called *teoatl,* meaning "Marvelous Water." **Grotesque birds:** buzzards and vultures.

The poet reads his flowery song
to the dead Axayácatl

Shadows of light and substance swirl on the mind
like red and dying leaves scattered in icy wind.

Our dead Mexica kings are frozen wood,
textured coarsely by memory, smoothed by starlight and time.

The last words the gods say make no sense.
The prayers are empty moonlight.

All our desires and illusions are grains of salt
washed away in a hail of rain.

Tizoc sparkles with gold and emeralds

The ancient priest with matted hair and long fingernails
emerges from rain clouds. His face is washed out like soggy maize;
his life is a flickering light. His mouth rings with no words,
yet he speaks to the snakes and scorpions.
He is not heard, but he charms jaguars.

The priest pierces the nose and ears of the new king with a maguey spine,
then inserts an emerald nose ring
and earplugs of gold.

The king, Tizoc, sits cross-legged on the royal mat,
padded with jaguar skins and quilted cotton.

His face glistens in golden dust and blood red pigment.

The eyes of the wizards sizzle as the breath of the gods
descends upon them.

The painters of history gasp at this splendor,
knowing their effigies and symbols
cannot capture this sunlight.

Tizoc: (pronounced: Tee-zohk) Mexica king, 1481-1486. Tizoc was the brother of Axayácatl and Ahuítzotl and the grandson of Motecuhzoma Ilhuicamina. The Spaniards
sometimes spelled the king's name, Tizocicatzin.

The sages and scribes cover their eyes as the king reads his poem

The poets come to Tenochtitlán in barges
across turquoise water dotted with chinampas
blooming in the morning sun.

Ambassadors from distant horizons,
dressed in rich plumage and sunlight,
cross the causeways to the music of flutes and conch shells.

Inside the city, sages and scribes cover their eyes
as Tizoc, our king and supreme poet,
prophesies Quetzalcóatl rising from the east
on his raft of serpents.

Tizoc recites his latest verse inside the royal aviaries
colored with the songs of scarlet tanagers,
blue and green macaws,
and delicate white egrets.

The king whispers his poem as the floating birds whistle:
I watch the turkey vultures tumbling in the sky, like black rain.

A heaven of vultures heaves overhead.
Those hideous birds wail all over the world,
filling men's hearts with a heavy dread.

The gods of peace and creation grieve like dying suns
as we wipe away our enemies like dust.

I have nothing left in my own heart
but pale moonlight and pain,
so encase my heart in worthless gold
and sink it in a sea of sorrow.

chinampas: raised garden beds of fruits and vegetables in Lake Texcoco. **I watch the turkey vultures tumbling in the sky, like black rain:** This poem reflects the piety and anti-war sentiments of Mexica King Tizoc (pronounced: Tee-zohk), who ruled from 1481-1486. Unlike most other Mexica kings, Tizoc was not enamored with combat, but with art and architecture. He was extremely pious, spending considerable time in contemplation inside Mexica temples. The lord of Tlacopan, a city on the western shore of Lake Texcoco, urged Tizoc at his installation as king of the Mexica to remain humble even as his subjects would revere him as an idol. The Tlacopan ruler said that a just and wise king appears poor among those who are needy, should commiserate with those who suffer, show strength and resolve to the mighty, and be severe with those who commit transgressions. Tizoc's aversion to warfare precipitated his assassination by the more hawkish members of the Mexica ruling elite who considered Tizoc a "lackluster" and timid ruler. Tizoc's undistinguished war record as king damaged the image of the Mexica military and encouraged brush fire rebellions across the empire. For instance, an insurrection in the Matlatzinca region was triggered in 1484 by the assassination of a Mexica tax collector *(calpixqui)* in the town of Tzinacantepec. The revolt was quelled, but Mexica warriors would be regularly mobilized, until the arrival of the Spaniards in 1519, to put down rebellions in the empire.

Those who must go on, are carried by the ancestors

Tizoc watches the sky:
he sees each light shining fitfully
as if every glimmering ember in the heavens
were right in front of his eyes.

He sees, perhaps, what moves
beyond the known world.

Our dying lord Tizoc separates lies from truth
as easily as one would cast wood
from pieces of amber.

But still he is dying;
every part of his body is dying.

Neither gold nor wisdom
can save him from his descent
into the silent kingdom of death.

Let Tizoc pass away.

Those who must go on,
are carried by the ancestors.

Tizoc: (pronounced: Tee-zohk) Mexica king, 1481-1486. Tizoc was the brother of Ax-ayácatl and Ahuítzotl and the grandson of Motecuhzoma Ilhuicamina. **Tizoc watches the sky:** As Tizoc came to power, Nezahualpilli, lord of Texcoco, counseled him to watch the stars to learn of dangers imperiling his kingdom. The new king was also advised to make regular penitential offerings to the war god and lord of the sun, Huitzilopochtli. The constellation Taurus, which the Mexica called *mamalhuaztli,* was vitally important in Náhuatl religious ceremonies, including the burning of copal incense three times each night.

The ink becomes effigies of song and mourning

Look upon the red and black ink borne across the pages of our holy books.
Our history is embalmed here.
The ink itself becomes effigies of sun and nopal,
moon and jade, song and mourning.

Our lord, Tizoc, is painted in that red and black ink:
Our king slopes forward from the woven mat.
His eyes are closed;
no speech scroll dances from his mouth.

In the distant years that will come long after us,
men will run their fingers across this history.
They will study this dried ink
and they will know that once a great king died.

In those strange and unknowable days,
Tizoc will yet be blessed by sun and moon.

Look upon the red and black ink borne across the pages of our holy books: The
Mexica sacred texts were painted in red and black ink, representing writing and wisdom. **Our king slopes forward from the woven mat:** In the *Codex Mendoza*, one of
the Mexica codices (or, sacred books), King Tizoc is depicted slumping forward from
his royal woven reed mat, his eyes closed, and no speech scroll emanating from the
mouth. This depiction indicated that the king had died.

The smoke from the king's cremation will not obscure the truth forever

2-House. 3-Rabbit. 4-Reed. 5-Flint. 6-House. 7-Rabbit.

The truth is a burden. It weighs heavily on us,
like a bereavement.

Whether tomorrow or the day after tomorrow,
the truth will be made naked.

We will know who assembled the sorcerers in the smoky dusk.

And we will know who told those wizards to arrange the stars
so that evil might insinuate itself in this land.

But if it was not by sorcery,
then who concocted the poison, and measured its strength,
so that a terrible toll was taken?

The smoke from the king's cremation
will not obscure the truth forever.

Tizoc: Mexica king, 1481-1486. His name (pronounced: Tee-zohk) means "Bloodletter" or "Blood-Stained Leg." Tizoc's name glyph in the codices is a leg covered with small red dots representing bloodletting (from the Náhuatl word *tesu,* bloodletter). Despite his gruesome name and his rank of general prior to his coronation as king of the Mexica, Tizoc had little interest in military affairs. Instead, Tizoc was interested in constructing new temples and shrines in the Mexica capital and secluding himself in his palace where he studied theology. During Tizoc's reign, the Templo Mayor (Great Temple) was enlarged, and completed under Tizoc's successor. Mexica craftsmen also fashioned an exquisite monument, called the Stone of Tizoc, which depicts vassals dominated by King Tizoc. As king, Tizoc led Mexica warriors into battle against the independent city-state of Metztitlán in the northern reaches of the empire. The campaign was a crushing defeat for the Mexica army, and Tizoc fled back to his capital while his soldiers were still fighting at Metztitlán. Tizoc's lack of concern for the military, combined with the defeat at the hands of Metztitlán, sparked a palace coup against the Mexica king in 1486.

Tizoc was poisoned, perhaps by order of his brother, Ahuítzotl, who succeeded him as king. According to some accounts, however, Tizoc's death was the result of sorcery. One account that perhaps confirms an unnatural death records that blood was gushing from the king's mouth as he was being carried on a litter from his palace, the day that he died. **The smoke from the king's cremation:** The bodies of Mexica rulers were cremated at death. **2-House. 3-Rabbit. 4-Reed. 5-Flint. 6-House. 7-Rabbit:** The years on the Mexica calendar in which Tizoc was king (the years 1481-1486 on the Christian calendar).

Tezcatlipoca censes a temple at night

This is a time of flux and change, this year 7-Rabbit,
when earthly things are scattered and kings assassinated.

Bowls of poison glisten in the moonlight,
and fury blossoms in men's hearts.

Birds drop from the sky as Tezcatlipoca censes a temple at night.

Our night lord knows that which must come.
He buries his ethereal thoughts inside the heads of necromancers.
Only they understand his dark sayings.

The stars hold their sway; we are held in their sway.

We are only painted effigies in a book,
whose pages must be wiped clean.

The truth is obscured like clouds gathered over a lake.

Tezcatlipoca: The god of night and material things. Tezcatlipoca was the patron of Mexica kings, who ruled at Tezcatlipoca's pleasure; at any time, for any reason, the god with the smoking mirror could depose the king. **7-Rabbit:** the Christian year 1486; the year Mexica King Tizoc was assassinated, perhaps by poisoning. **necromancers:** those skilled in divination by communicating with the dead. **his dark sayings:** mysterious utterances. **The stars hold their sway:** the stars influenced the destinies of mortals. **We are only painted effigies:** A prayer addressed to Tezcatlipoca expresses the Mexica acknowledgement of the brevity of life: "Only as painted figures in your book / Have we lived here on the earth. . . . We were no more than pictures / Rubbed out, erased." **The truth is obscured like clouds gathered over a lake:** Tezcatlipoca carried the title Tezcatlanextia, meaning "He Who Causes Things to Be Seen in the Mirror." The god's smoky mirror "clouds up all over like shadows on its surface."

Ahuítzotl's first pronouncement at court

The king is a beast,
whose words like sulphurous clouds
overwhelm both body and soul.

The king sits at the pleasure of no one.
His will is not ratified.
His will is said and done.

By force, he rules. He rules by fear.

The people do not know him.
They are dumbstruck by his face seared into the sun
and painted across the moon.

Who are my people, but bees?
They are busy in their hives, momentarily.
Then, they are gone,
and no memory of them remains.

But the king dies, and his passion burns in the blood-red moon.

The king is a beast: Ahuítzotl, Mexica king, 1486-1502. Ahuítzotl's name means the "Water Beast—which the Mexica depicted as a furry, mythical animal with pointed ears, raccoon-like hands, and a long tail. It had some similarities to an otter and other characteristics of an opossum. The magical creature was believed to be the cause of death by drowning. Ahuítzotl was elected king when he was in school and without any experience in combat. Newly installed Mexica kings were expected to personally lead their soldiers into battle in coronation wars. Ahuítzotl's inaugural war was a series of battles against cities that had been rebellious in recent years, particularly in the region of Chiapas, and proved the new king to be a valiant commander of men. The Spaniards sometimes spelled the king's name, Ahuítzotzin. **By force, he rules. He rules by fear:** Ahuítzotl's fierce personality buttressed a government that ruled by force and terror. Ahuítzotl was revered as a *teuctlamacazqui*—a high priest who bore the image of the ferocious god Huitzilopochtli on his shoulder. Ahuítzotl supervised the completion of the Great Temple (Templo Mayor), a massive pyramid with two shrines on its summit, one to Huitzilopochtli, god of war and lord of the sun, and Tláloc, god of rain and fertility. To commemorate the completion of the Great Temple in 1487, a large-scale sacrifice of slaves and prisoners of war was conducted at the summit of the pyramid. According to some Spanish sources, the Mexica sacrificed as many as 80,000 victims over a four-day period. To many modern scholars, that number seems ridiculously high. In fact, the Spanish chroniclers may have accidentally or deliberately exaggerated the numbers of sacrificial victims to emphasize the "paganism" and "barbarism" of the "Indians." Between 1491 and 1495, Ahuítzotl led the Mexica army to the Pacific, seizing coastal lands from Acapulco to Zacatula. The great Mexica conqueror also commanded military campaigns against Oaxaca in 1488-1489 and 1494-1495 and into the Isthmus of Tehuantepec in 1496. Ahuítzotl's last major war was waged against the Soconusco (Xoconochco) region, near the border of Guatemala. Ahuítzotl took his warriors as far as 700 miles from the Mexica capital, and they penetrated into those distant realms without the benefit of horses or pack animals. His overbearing personality endures in the Mexican-Spanish word *ahuízote,* meaning a violent, vindictive, and fierce person.

Violet moons hiss in the deepest part of the sea

Stone towers rise from the lake,
the handsome heads of proud cranes.

Stone temples have stood since the beginning of time.

Who cut this stone from silence,
made magnificence from shadow?

From still and blue waters that run deeper than the memories of the gods,
Ahuítzotl emerges,
shaking his head in the brilliant sun.

His eyes flame like violet moons hissing
in the deepest part of the sea.

Ahuítzotl, the Water Beast, breaks clouds upon the rocks.
A terrible rumbling blossoms furiously across the sky.
The water crashes in torrents.

Ahuítzotl sinks his hands into the wooden cribs
filled with maize and beans.
The great speaker knows this is his final feast.

Ahuítzotl and the bearer of years disappear together
into the twilight.

Ahuítzotl's flesh and blood become shiny stone.

Ahuítzotl: (pronounced: Ah-weet-zoh-tl) Mexica king, 1486-1502. Ahuítzotl was the brother of Tizoc and Axayácatl and grandson of Motecuhzoma Ilhuicamina. Ahuítzotl was a high-ranking military officer *(tlacatecatl)* and a high priest. He was a forbidding, peremptory ruler, whose personality was charismatic. **Stone towers rise from the lake:** Tenochtitlán was a city built on an island in the middle of Lake Texcoco, with three straight and level stone causeways leading to the city from the mainland. The city boasted magnificent stone pyramids, towers, and buildings and shrines and statues to the great deities. The Mexica constructed palaces made of stone and cedar wood containing spacious rooms with windows covered in awnings of woven cotton. The Spaniards, led by Hernán Cortés, were mesmerized by the city on the lake when they first arrived there in 1519. The conquistador and historian Bernal Diaz wrote: "When we saw many towns and villages constructed on the water and other towns on the dry land and that great road on the embankment that led to Mexico, so straight and flat, we were astounded as they were like the enchantments we read about in legend, with the great towers and buildings rising from the water, all built of stone. And our soldiers asked themselves if all those things they saw were just a dream." King Ahuítzotl was a patron of the arts, who loved to hear poets recite their verses and music performed in his palace. **Ahuítzotl's flesh and bones become stone:** Ahuítzotl ordered a second, six-mile long aqueduct constructed to channel water from mainland springs at Coyoacan to Tenochtitlán. The king was advised against the project because of the possibility of flooding inside the capital. But Ahuítzotl dismissed those concerns and work on the great hydraulic project began. When the aqueduct was completed, Ahuítzotl himself threw golden objects, fashioned as fishes and frogs, into the flowing waters. The earlier reservations about flooding were not unfounded. The water flow from Coyoacan was so substantial that the level of Lake Texcoco rose, flooding many cultivated chinampas along the shores of the island city. The waters continued to rise perilously, inundating Tenochtitlán itself before Mexica engineers and workers checked the water flow from the mainland source. Vast areas of the capital city had to be rebuilt after the Great Flood and Ahuítzotl himself died in 1502 (the Mexica year 10-Rabbit), a short time after striking his head on a stone lintel or doorjamb in the royal palace while trying to flee from the flood. It was an ironic death for a king whose name means "Water Beast." However, the Spanish Catholic friar and historian Father Diego Durán recorded that Ahuítzotl had contracted an intestinal virus during a military campaign in the tropics of southern Mexico. Fr. Durán wrote that the malady emaciated the king so that he looked nearly "flesh-less" just before he died.

Ahuítzotl is smoke trailing the sun

Ahuítzotl was born miraculously of that water
that is like a whirlpool that never stops moving
as if it were the sea itself.

Descendant of stormy weather,
Ahuítzotl was divine, imperial, ferocious.

He was our lord, he of the great voice,
resident in the house of gold and amber,
multicolored cotton,
and cacao of different colors.

His voice thundered.
He moved like a tremor in the earth.

Our Water Beast terrified us
until that day when his light dimmed,
and was deadened.

What is left of our king?
Where is his flesh and voice?

Perhaps he is embalmed in the sky,
crystallized in sunlight,
or he is smoke forever trailing the sun.

Ahuítzotl: Mexica king, 1486-1502. **of that water that is like a whirlpool:** a Nahua description of raging water. **he of the great voice:** A Mexica ruler was known as the *huei tlatoani* (pronounced: ooeh tlah-toh-ah-ni) or, great speaker, or, he of the great voice. **Our Water Beast terrified us:** Ahuítzotl's name glyph in the codices depicts a fierce water animal *(ahuítzotl)* with a stream of water running down the creature's back and tail. The name, Ahuítzotl, roughly translates into "Water Beast." King Ahuítzotl was a fierce warrior and a harsh and often impetuous ruler, who governed by force and terror. Under Ahuítzotl's rule, the Mexica government dramatically increased the scale of human sacrifices to instill fear in the masses and to demonstrate reverence to the Mexica deities. Ahuítzotl restored the military reputation of the Mexica empire that had suffered under his two predecessors. He launched wide-ranging military campaigns that nearly doubled the territory under Mexica domination.

The Mexica survey the world

The nearest cities have brought their baskets of cacao ground with maize flour.
Bins of chia. Bins of amaranth.

Here are the tiles of fine gold, copper bells, and bins of lime
from the conquered kingdoms.

Envoys from provinces far afield will bring us
large green stones, round, like tomatoes.

Our subjects prosper from defense and trade,
which we provide as readily as the sun gives its rays.

But the meddlesome Tlaxcaltecas are tardy
in delivering their tribute.

They make bold statements each time this year,
refining their arrogance to an artisan's craft.

Their lords live lavishly in stone palaces
and regard themselves as devout and prayerful,
but they speak in questions
and bare the truth to riddles.

Let that pride be punished by swift chastisement;
rebellion is always broken like soft rock.

---

cacao ground with maize flour: called, in Náhuatl, *cacahuapinoli*. For an account of
Mexica-Tlaxcalteca hostilities, please see the poem, "The frenzy of men is no interest to
the gods." **large green stones, round, like tomatoes:** a description written by Spanish Fray Bernardino de Sahagún, in the *Florentine Codex,* IX, ch. 4.

The tlapalizquixochitl tree

Motecuhzoma Xocoyotzin measured the light and heat glowing from the sun.
He turned opaque omens into shadows crowding into broken temples.

The king bowed his head before fate and astrology,
his heart hardened by thorny days.

The people of many enemy towns
had sharp words ululating from their mouths.

An embassy was sent to Tlachquiachco,
but our ambassadors were chased away in haste.

So our priests blew their conch shells like thunder.
And the Mexica warriors painted their faces in red and black.
They put on their feathers, bells, and bracelets
and ran into war, waving the egret banners,
shaking the yucca seed rattles,
and firing barbed and deadly darts.

Temples with thatched roofs were burned
as smoking emblems blew across the sky.

We had conquered our enemy, destroyed them,
and served the sun and gave it a drink.

But the spoils of war only withered in our hands.

Motecuhzoma Xocoyotzin: (pronounced: Maw-tay-kwah-SOH-mah Shoh-koh-yoh-tzin) (*c.*1468-1520) Mexica great speaker, 1502-1520. Sometimes his name is pronounced, "Mohk-the-ZOO-mah." **The tlapalizquixochitl tree:** In 1503, Motecuhzoma Xocoyotzin received reports of a small but beautiful tropical *tlapalizquixochitl* tree bearing fragrant blossoms and delicious fruits that Malinal, the Mixtec king of Tlachquiachco, had imported from a tropic region. Motecuhzoma Xocoyotzin enjoyed vanilla orchid plants, cacao trees, and other exotic species, but he was chagrined that Malinal's tree was not beautifying one of his botanical gardens. (The tree probably would not have survived in the cold winter climate of the Mexica capital). After Malinal refused repeated demands to turn over the tree to Mexica tribute gatherers, Motecuh-zoma Xocoyotzin sent his army to Tlachquiachco. Malinal and many of his subjects died in the defense of their city, which was incorporated into the Mexica empire. **But the spoils of war only withered in our hands:** The little tree was uprooted and died en route to Tenochtitlán. **We had conquered our enemy, destroyed them, / and served the sun and gave it a drink:** quotation from the *Codex Chimalpopoca*.

The frenzy of men is no interest to the gods

The divinities, sleekly beautiful in obsidian and shell,
enter our collective dream mournfully.

They wait impatiently for the frenzied scattering
of demigods speaking foreign tongues
and the burning of enemy temples.

The Mexica armies turn stone and sky blue temples
into a whirlwind of smoke perpetually clearing away.

So the Tlaxcaltecas are crowded together like quails in a cage.

They gawk at strange omens
floating above their heads.

Their prayers and incantations are dispersed
like falling waters.

Their treasury is starved of cacao and cotton.

No gold glitters like the sea.

Even Huixtocihuatl has fled to the netherworld,
so that all the grains of salt in Tlaxcala
are washed away like the moon's light at dawn.

The days are being washed away.

The Tlaxcaltecas run here and there,
with their hands urgently flailing in the sky.

But the frenzy of men is no interest to the gods.

---

the Tlaxcaltecas are crowded together like quails in a cage: As early as Axayácatl's reign (1469-1481), the province of Tlaxcala emerged as the principal threat to Mexica dominance in the Valley of Mexico. For years the Mexica had blockaded Tlaxcala, preventing the importation into the rival principality of cotton, precious metals, tropical feathers, cacao, and salt. Beginning in the 1470s, during the period of encirclement, the Mexica waged intermittent "wars of flowers" against Tlaxcala, seizing prisoners of war to be sacrificed atop shrines in the Mexica capital. Motecuhzoma Xocoyotzin declared that his predecessors had been content to keep the Tlaxcaltecas ensnared within Mexica territory "like quails in a cage," a dependable source of sacrificial victims to be captured in ritual "wars of flowers." Motecuhzoma quickly demonstrated that more aggressive forms of combat would replace mere flowery wars and economic encirclement. In 1504, Motecuhzoma decided to dispense with the "war of flowers" and prosecute a full-blown "war of arrows" against the Tlaxcaltecas. But the Tlaxcaltecas, fighting in their own homeland, enjoyed advantages in intelligence and communications, resupply, and knowledge of terrain. It is unclear whether Motecuhzoma Xocoyotzin sought to annex Tlaxcala to his empire or to extinguish Tlaxcalteca autonomy by making the rival province a satellite. Motecuhzoma Xocoyotzin failed to attain either one of these objectives. Perhaps Motecuhzoma Xocoyotzin, his ministers, and the Mexica military high command underestimated the resolve and resourcefulness of Tlaxcala, which was a powerful and vast league of towns and cities in the Pueblo-Tlaxcala Valley. Like the Tarascans in Axayácatl's day, the Tlaxcaltecas fought tenaciously to preserve their independence. When the Spaniards arrived at Tlaxcala in 1519, they observed the hatred with which the Tlaxcaltecas held the Mexica, as a result of the prolonged war and the economic debilitation caused by the Mexica blockade.

Between 1505 and 1515, the Mexica and Tlaxcaltecas settled into an uneasy truce, or more accurately, a stalemate. However, in 1515 war erupted between Tlaxcala and the province of Huexotzinco, a powerful kingdom with a tradition of military strength and independence dating back to the thirteenth century. Perhaps hoping to benefit from Tlaxcalteca distraction, Motecuhzoma Xocoyotzin ordered an invasion of Tlaxcala. But with the impending Mexica assault, the Tlaxcaltecas and Huexotzinca hastily repaired the rift between their two provinces, allying themselves together against the Mexica, who were routed. Many Mexica warriors were slain and their leading commanders were taken by the Tlaxcaltecas as prisoners of war. Motecuhzoma Xocoyotzin was enraged at the reports that his army had been routed at Tlaxcala. He berated the surviving commanders once they had returned to the Mexica capital. The king fumed: "How have you succumbed in this effeminate manner, that I should be shamed before all the world? To what end did so many brave lords and captains go forth, so trained and experienced in war? Is it possible that they have forgotten how to order and reinforce their ranks, to break through an enemy? I can only believe that you have been purposely slothful, to strike a blow at myself and make fun of me." Motecuhzoma Xocoyotzin decreed that no mourning be displayed and no honors bestowed upon the returning, defeated commanders and warriors. The king also ordered that the generals involved in the defeat be stripped of their insignia, barred from wearing prestigious cotton and sandals, and ostracized them from the royal palace for one year. In the wake of the defeat, Motecuhzoma Xocoyotzin tightened military discipline within the Mexica ranks. The long period of wars of flowers and wars of arrows developed the Tlaxcaltecas into seasoned warriors. In 1519, the Tlaxcaltecas and Huexotzinca allied themselves with Cortés's Spanish army. They exerted a major role in the defeat of the Mexica empire. Some Mexicans today claim that the Tlaxcaltecas betrayed the indigenous Mexicans during the Spanish conquest. Of course, that is not how the Tlaxcaltecas view history. As the distinguished Tlaxcalteca muralist Desidero Xochitiotzin has argued, his ancestors fought alongside the Spaniards, and against the Mexica, so that Tlaxcala would not disappear from the map, vanishing from history. **Huixtocihuatl:** Mexica goddess of salt. The derivation of the name is uncertain other than her close identification with the salty water of the sea.

Only a little while here

All the stars are slaves to the moon,
that large millstone,
burning very round and very red.

But the moon is not in the heavens forever.
Only a little while there.

Motecuhzoma Xocoyotzin, our reverent lord,
is anointed with divine pigment
and crowned with turquoise diadem and moonlight.

In a whisper, he speaks in rumbling thunder.
He possesses sunlight and storm.
He holds yellow ovals and stark white crescents.
Everything he has shines with lime.

He eats of chile peppers, tomatoes, and green ears of corn,
shelled ears of corn.

Birds of rich plumage serenade Motecuhzoma
as the sun burns through the clouds.

His armies cover the fields,
like the waves of the sea.

But still his warriors fall to the Tlaxcaltecas,

who come crouching, whistling and yelling,
shaking their heads,
making a great clamor as they come.

The Mexica warriors become rain clearing at dusk.
Their feathered staffs have been thrown away.
Their obsidian arms and decorated shields are scattered
like kernels of maize.

The glory is passing away.
The lime is washing away.

Everything is only a dream.

For this moment only, Motecuhzoma is our king.
Only a little while in this house of coarse cloth and cotton,
jade, gold, and quetzal feathers.

The rays of the sun are descending
into the kingdom of skulls and bones.

And when the sun sets,
it gives its light only to the dead.

Our home is not upon the earth.
Only a little while here.

---

the moon, that large millstone, burning very round and very red: a Mexica description of the moon. **Motecuhzoma Xocoyotzin:** (pronounced: Maw-tay-kwah-SOH-mah Shoh-koh-yoh-tzin) (*c.*1468-1520) Mexica great speaker, 1502-1520. He was the son of Axayácatl and nephew of Ahuítzotl. When he ascended to the Mexica throne in 1502 at the age of thirty-four or thirty-five, Motecuhzoma Xocoyotzin was already noted for his military valor, political abilities, and profound religious piety. He was also a philosopher and astrologer, who had a deep appreciation for Mexica art. As a young man, Motecuhzoma had studied for the priesthood. Like Tizoc, Motecuhzoma Xocoyotzin was extremely pious. Immediately after his coronation, Motecuhzoma Xocoyotzin did days of penitence to please the deities. He was a wise, prudent, often introspective ruler who possessed a gift of eloquent oratory. One account holds: "When he spoke, he drew the sympathy of others by his subtle phrases and seduced them by his profound reasoning."

The Spaniards sometimes spelled the king's name, Moteuczomatzin Xocoyotzin. **turquoise diadem:** the blue triangular diadem was a symbol of lordly power. **In a whisper, he speaks like a rumbling thunder:** It was said that Motecuhzoma spoke just above a whisper. Many considered him to be the most eloquent of all Mexica rulers, even though he was a cold and distant figure, lacking the enormous charisma of his predecessor, Ahuítzotl. Motecuhzoma Xocoyotzin had a sense of humor; on occasion he would laugh or "giggle helplessly," and at times he could appear benevolent. However, he was especially noted for his solemnity and inflexibility. He was a proud man who was feared by the vassals of the Mexica empire and by his own people. Like other Mexica kings who had ruled before him, Motecuhzoma appeared in public only during urgent occasions. When he did make a public appearance, the king would not walk on unswept ground and he commanded the awe of spectators. During one appearance in the capital, the crowd became so still at Motecuhzoma Xocoyotzin's passing, that "all heads were bowed, so that it seemed that the multitude was hardly alive at all." **He holds yellow ovals and stark white crescents:** nose and headdress ornaments, symbolizing divinity. **the sun burns through the clouds:** In Náhuatl symbolism, Motecuhzoma's name means, tellingly: "Sun Burning Through the Clouds." **His armies cover the fields, / like the waves of the sea:** In 1503, a year after his election as king, Motecuhzoma Xocoyotzin dispatched warriors to subjugate the town of Achiutla. He personally led Mexica warriors toward the Mixtec frontier of Tototepec, rich in goods and stretched along the Pacific coast of Oaxaca. In 1507, the centers of Yanhuitlan and Zozollan, heartened by the Mexica defeat, rose in rebellion that saw Mexica merchants and tax collectors murdered. Motecuhzoma Xocoyotzin unleashed punitive raids to crush the insurrections. Deploying overwhelming force (perhaps as many as 200,000 warriors), the Mexica wiped out the townspeople of Yanhuitlan and burned their homes. Meanwhile, the inhabitants of Zozollan deserted their city, finding refuge in the mountains, so that they would avoid the slaughter that had befallen the people of Yanhuitlan. After a four-day search, the Mexica army could find no one from Zozollan to punish. In 1508, Motecuhzoma Xocoyotzin challenged Cholula to a war of flowers. The Mexica triumphed and the Cholulans declared themselves to be allies of Motecuhzoma. Two years later, a zodiacal light flared, supposedly igniting additional revolts throughout the empire. In 1510, Motecuhzoma brutally crushed a rebellion by the Zulantlacas who had risen against Mexica tax gatherers. Whether actually precipitated by the meteorological phenomena or not, the Tlachquiauca people, who had suffered a war with the Mexica over a fruit tree in 1503 (please see the poem "The tlapalizquixochitl tree"), again attempted to resist Motecuhzoma Xocoyotzin's authority. In 1511, the Tlachquiauca refused to pay their tributary obligations and obstructed Mexica trade from the Pacific coast and the Isthmus of Tehuantepec. The insurrection at Tlachquiauhco was quickly put down and 12,210 captives were taken to be sacrificed. **But still his warriors fall to the Tlaxcaltecas:** Beginning in 1504, Motecuhzoma Xocoyotzin renewed the flowery wars against the independent city-state of Tlaxcala (pronounced: Tlash-Kah-la). Please see the poems, "The buzzards are gathering, thickly, in the sky" and "The frenzy of men is no interest to the gods." Most scholars contend that the Mexica fought the wars against the Tlaxcaltecas not to subjugate them or conquer territory, but to capture prisoners to sacrifice in the name of the Mexica war god, Huitzilopochtli. Please see the poem "Huitzilopochtli, in the beginning and in the end." However, many Mexica accounts reveal Motecuhzoma Xocoyotzin's resolute determination to crush Tlaxcala. In 1515, war erupted between Tlaxcala and the province of Huexotzinco, a powerful kingdom with a tradition of military strength and independence dating back to the thirteenth century. Perhaps hoping to benefit from Tlaxcalteca distraction, Motecuhzoma Xocoyotzin ordered an invasion of Tlaxcala. But with the impending Mexica assault, the Tlaxcaltecas and Huexotzinca hastily repaired the rift between their two provinces, allying themselves together against the Mexica, who were routed. Many Mexica warriors were slain and their leading commanders were taken by the Tlaxcaltecas as prisoners of war. The defeat was a serious indication of Mexica military vulnerability only four years before the arrival of Hernán Cortés and the Spanish conquistadores. Motecuhzoma Xocoyotzin was enraged at the reports that his army had been routed at Tlaxcala. He berated the surviving commanders once they had returned to the Mexica capital. The king fumed: "How have you succumbed in this effeminate manner, that I should be shamed before all the world? To what end did so many brave lords and captains go forth, so trained and experienced in war? Is it possible that they have forgotten how to order and reinforce their ranks, to break through an enemy? I can only believe that you have been purposely slothful, to strike a blow at myself and make fun of me." Motecuhzoma Xocoyotzin decreed that no mourning be displayed and no honors bestowed upon the returning, defeated commanders and warriors. The king also ordered that the generals involved in the defeat be stripped of their insignia, barred from wearing prestigious cotton and sandals, and ostracized them from the royal palace for one year. In the wake of the defeat, Motecuhzoma Xocoyotzin tightened military discipline within the Mexica ranks. The long period of wars of flowers and wars of arrows developed the Tlaxcaltecas into seasoned warriors. The defeat was a serious indication of Mexica military vulnerability only four years before the arrival of Hernán Cortés and the Spanish conquistadores. In 1519, the Tlaxcaltecas and Huexotzinca allied themselves with Cortés's Spanish army. They exerted a major role in the defeat of the Mexica empire. **obsidian arms:** obsidian-edged wooden clubs. **jade, gold, and quetzal feathers:** symbols of the materials most cherished by the Mexica. **Our home is not upon the earth. Only a little while here:** Mexica theology held that human existence on earth was mysterious and transitory. The Mexica believed that time and the universe were measured by epochs, or suns, and were subject largely to the desires of the cosmic deities. The Mexica believed that four previous suns had ended disastrously, and the present sun would be the last. The Mexica understood that the sun would be extinguished by a cataclysmic wind, or by a series of massive earthquakes that would swallow everything on the earth while the stars, including the sun, would be shaken down from the sky. Perhaps the sun would just set and never rise again. Even the powerful Mexica kings were not considered to be immortal, nor were their accomplishments regarded as eternal. Like other mortals, once their fleeting moment on earth was over, Mexica kings traveled to the silent kingdom of the dead, called Mictlán, the "Place where no smoke escapes, the place of no chimney," where "not once more will [he] make [his] return." The ephemeral nature of life and fortune was captured by a Mexica scribe, who recounted the disintegration of the beautiful home of an affluent merchant: "There all would answer the calls of nature—would urinate and defecate—and rubbish would be cast. Salts would lie evaporated; and the earth would lie smoldering. Then it would be said, and so that all might marvel: 'Once, in this place, here, was the house of one who came commanding reverence. Here came a householder enjoying fame; there was always honor, and the house was swept clean. At least the rubbish was cast aside somewhere. And none might urinate on his walls or he would chide them. But now in this very place only the walls remain standing.'" **the kingdom of bones and skulls:** Mictlán. Unlike the Christian conception of the underworld as a place of punishment, Mictlán was the place where the souls of the dead found eternal rest.

13-Rabbit

The wind rises from the edges of the earth.

The skies divide like rushing waters
as dark clouds heave from horizon to horizon.

The remains of the ancestors leach away in the rain.

In these final months,
ancient tongues and prayers sing untrammeled
in the tenuous solitude.

13-Rabbit: The Mexica year 13-Rabbit corresponded to the Christian year Anno Domini 1518. This poem depicts an unspecified place in the Valley of Mexico in 13-Rabbit, the year before the arrival of Hernán Cortés and the Spaniards in Tenochtitlán.

The Mexica scribes saw what they saw

The Mexica scribes saw what they saw.
They drew their sightings in the painted books
that contain every fragment of truth.

The scribes were the witnesses of that streamer of light
whirling and arcing in a year not marked sacred by the priests,
a brilliant brightness leaping from the earth to the heavens,
a cascade of light bathing both gods and beasts
in resplendence as sparkling as gold.

And so the contemplative men studied the stars and dice,
they read the numerology,
weighed the omens, gray and black,
and told us how their minds were swayed.

Where are they now,
those men who had facts stuffed inside their heads?

Why have they abandoned us in our grief?

---

that streamer of light: a zodiacal light that flared in 1509. **the omens, gray and black, / and told us how their minds were swayed:** a famine in 1505, a plague of rats in 1506, the appearance of zodiacal light in 1509, snow in 1512, and earthquakes in 1512 and 1513.

The soothsayer traces a pall around the moon

The soothsayer sees a darkening hue, like a pall,
circling around the moon.

He plucks flowers made of ice,
weeping over harbingers hanging in the heavens,
portending the end of the world.

A comet, like a tongue of fire, a dart of fire, a flaming ear of corn,
bleeds fire, drop by drop,
like a terrible wound in the eastern sky.

The rushing fireball heaves ice into the very depths of men's souls.

The people clap their hands against their mouths.
They are staggered and dumbstruck.
They ask themselves what that fiery signal could mean.

Princes and priests wash their hands in ancient religious light
flickering now at the end of the world.

Motecuhzoma Xocoyotzin shivers in the wind blown cold off the moon.

The soothsayer, the wise man, in whose hands rest the books: a description in the Florentine Codex. The moon here refers to Mexico, whose name derives from the Náhuatl name Metztli, the moon-deity, from which Mexico (pronounced "Mescico" by natives) means full moon, or "Where the Moon Appears." **A comet, like a tongue of fire:** In 1517, two years before the arrival of the Spaniards, a comet appeared above Tenochtitlán. According to one account recorded by the Spanish priest Fray Bernardino de Sahagún, the comet appeared in broad daylight as "a fiery signal, like a flaming ear of corn or the blaze of daybreak; it seemed to bleed fire, drop by drop, like a wound in the sky. . .it shone in the very heart of the heavens." Sahagún further wrote: "This great marvel caused so much dread and wonder that [the Mexica] spoke of it constantly trying to imagine what such a strange novelty could signify." **Motecuhzoma Xocoyotzin shivers in the wind blown cold off the moon:** according to postconquest accounts, Motecuhzoma was devastated by omens portending the collapse of his empire. The Spaniards undoubtedly manufactured these accounts so that the Mexica king would be seen not as an heroic figure, but as ruler imprisoned by idolatry and pagan superstition.

The bird in the color of ashes

A wondrous bird in the color of ashes,
an ashen-hued bird, like a crane,
with a strange, smoking mirror in the crown of its head,
stares at Motecuhzoma Xocoyotzin
as if all the knowledge in the world
dances inside the bird's brain.

The great speaker, adorned in a headdress of quetzal feathers,
stands speechless as the bird fills the palace with a wailing song.

What does this sorrow song mean?
This creature, what does it know?

Motecuhzoma Xocoyotzin stretches out his arms to the bird,
which now takes its awkward strides forward.

The bird, painted as if in ash, bends toward our king,
who peers into the cloudy mirror gleaming in the creature's head.

Motecuhzoma gasps to see the stars shining in the firmament.

But how can these stars dance in the mirror
when now it is broad daylight?

Motecuhzoma glances away,
then returns the long stare into the looking glass.

The stars are gone, each one.
Daylight fills the obsidian mirror
as strange men, fully bearded,
mounted on deer high as houses,
ride up from the sea.

The foreigners sweep across a distant plain,
spread out in ranks,

and coming forward in great haste.

Here and there are fires and many ruins swirling.

Motecuhzoma closes his eyes,
and the miraculous bird vanishes.

You soothsayers, you clairvoyant priests,
you wisest men among us,
can you say what these signs portend?

A wondrous bird in the color of ashes: According to a Spanish account, undoubtedly fabricated, Mexica fisherman snared a miraculous ashen-colored bird carrying the
god Tezcatlipoca's smoking obsidian mirror on its head. The bird was caught in a canal
in Tenochtitlán and taken to the royal palace. The Mexica great speaker Motecuhzoma
Xocoyotzin (pronounced: Maw-tay-kwah-SOH-mah Shoh-koh-yoh-tzin) was said to
have gazed into the bird's magical obsidian mirror and beheld the glittering stars of *mamalhuaztli* (the constellation Taurus) in the daylight sky and the Spanish conquistadores marching towards the Mexica capital. For information on Tezcatlipoca, please see
the poem, "Lord of the smoking mirror." **You soothsayers, you clairvoyant priests:**
Soothsayers, wizards, astrologers, augurs, oracles, illusionists, and sorcerers and their
prognostications deeply affected all aspects of Mexica society—the sacred and secular,
public and private, common and ruling classes.

Pyramids floating on the sea

The Year 12-House

The spies have returned to us from strange frontiers
with unusual news in their mouths.

These trustworthy men have seen pyramids floating on the sea,
bringing strangers dressed on all sides with metal,
leaving only their dead white faces exposed.
They have faces white as chalk,
and their hair is yellow like the sun.

These aliens pray in a harsh and unknowable tongue
to strange gods whose heads are enveloped in light.

Their deer carry them wherever they want to go.

These strange-looking deer are as high
as the terraces of houses.

The deer are fitted with little bells that ring and clamor as they gallop.

The deer themselves snort and foam,
making loud noises when they run,
like stones raining down on the earth.

Wherever the deer run, they make the earth tremble,
as if the world were caught in a fit of vertigo.
Their hooves leave pits and scars on the ground.

The strange men have enormous dogs, with flattened ears
and tongues that dangle hideously from their mouths.
The color of their eyes is a violent yellow.
Their eyes burn with fire.

These dogs bound here and there, panting all the while,

with their tongues hanging out ravenously.
These four-legged devils are spotted like an ocelot.

And the foreigners have tubes of fire that bellow like thunder,
overtaking and deafening men's ears.

The tubes shoot out balls of stone,
scattering sparks and raining fire.
The smoke is foul, having a fetid stench like rotten mud
that verily wounds the head.

And when the ball of stone strikes a mountain,
the mountain seems to fall apart and crumble.
And when it strikes a tree, the tree splinters and vanishes,
as if someone has blown it away.

Pyramids floating on the sea: In the Mexica year 12-House (or, 1517 on the Christian calendar), a peasant informed Motecuhzoma Xocoyotzin that he had seen a great mountain floating on the sea. The peasant, in fact, had seen a Spanish ship commanded by Francisco Hernández de Córdoba that had reached the Yucatán coast. The Spaniards were amazed by a Mayan settlement on Cabo Catoche, now identified with the archaeological site at Ecab. Christened "El Gran Cairo" by the newcomers, the center boasted temples and shrines which the Spaniards called *mezquitas,* or "mosques," houses of stone, mortar, and thatched roofs, streets, squares, and a marketplace. From the Córdoba expedition, the Spaniards compiled their first accounts of the Yucatán peninsula. The following year, Juan de Grijalva led three ships from Cuba to explore the Yucatán. Sailing from the island of Cozumel, north of the modern-day port of Vera Cruz, to the Río Pánuco, the Spanish mariners observed the snow-capped peaks of Mexican volcanoes. Grijalva and his men realized that the Yucatán was an immense country rather than an island or group of islands, as the Spaniards had earlier believed. Motecuhzoma Xocoyotzin's tribute-gatherers on the coast greeted the visitors, presenting them with cotton fabrics and receiving handfuls of glass beads in return. In 1519, a flotilla of eleven Spanish ships, commanded by Hernán Cortés arrived at the Yucatán. Mexica spies rushed reports back to Tenochtitlán of Spanish armored warriors, horses, huge man-killing mastiff dogs, swords, muskets, and cannons. This poem is based on the Mexica accounts of the Córdoba, Grijalva, and Cortés expeditions, incorporating some of the Mexica descriptions. Motecuhzoma's spies, sent to keep watch on the foreigners, described their appearance for the emperor: "They dress in metal; they cover their heads with metal, the swords are metal, their bows are metal, their shields are metal, the lances are metal. And those that carry them on their backs—the deer—seem as high as the terraces of houses. They cover their bodies on all sides, leaving only their dead white faces exposed; they have faces as white as chalk. They have yellow hair. Some, however, have black hair; their beards are long and yellow." The envoys also described the dust that rose in a whirlwind on the roads from hooves of horses and the boots of men in battle array: "It was as if the earth trembled beneath them, or as if the world were spinning. . .as it spins during a fit of vertigo." Messengers rushed reports of the cannon fire to Moctecuhzoma, telling him of the Spaniards' dreadful fire-breathing weapon: "how it resounded like thunder when it went off. Indeed, it overpowered one: it deafened our ears. And when it discharged, something like a round of pellet came from within. Fire went scattered forth; sparks showered forth. And its smoke smelled very foul; it had a fetid odor which verily wounded the head. And when [the pellet] struck [a] mountain, [it was] as if it fell apart and crumbled. And when it struck a tree, it splintered, seeming to vanish as if someone blew it away." Later, when the Spaniards approached the palace at Tenochtitlán, they repeatedly shot off their guns. A Mexica chronicler wrote that the Spanish guns "exploded, sputtered, thundered. Smoke spread, it grew dark with smoke, every place filled with smoke." Mexica scribes recorded another version of the description of the foreigners: "A thing like a ball of stone comes out of its entrails: it comes out shooting sparks and raining fire. The smoke that comes out with it has a pestilent odor, like that of rotten mud. This odor penetrates even to the brain and causes the greatest discomfort. If the cannon is aimed against a mountain, the mountain splits and cracks open. If it is aimed against a tree, it shatters the tree into splinters. This is a most unnatural sight, as if the tree had exploded from within. Their trappings and arms are all made of iron. They dress in iron and wear iron casques on their heads. Their swords are iron; their bows are iron; their shields are iron; their spears are iron. Their deer carry them on their backs wherever they wish to go. These deer, our lord, are as tall as the roof of a house. The strangers' bodies are completely covered, so that only their faces can be seen. Their skin is white, as if it were made of lime. They have yellow hair, though some of them have black. Their beards are long and yellow, and their moustaches are also yellow. Their hair is curly, with very fine strands. As for their food, it is like human food. It is large and white, and not heavy. It is something like straw, but with the taste of a cornstalk, of the pith of a cornstalk. It is a little sweet, as if it were flavored with honey; it tastes of honey, it is sweet-tasting food. Their dogs are enormous, with flat ears and long, dangling tongues. The color of their eyes is a burning yellow; their eyes flash fire and shoot off sparks. Their bellies are hollow, their flanks long and narrow. They are tireless and very powerful. They bound here and there panting, with their tongues hanging out. And they are spotted like an ocelot." Yet another scribe colorfully described the Spanish horses: "These deer wear little bells, they are adorned with many little bells. When the deer gallop, the bells make a loud clamor, ringing and reverberating. These deer snort and bellow. They sweat a very great deal, the sweat pours from their bodies in streams. The foam from their muzzles drips onto the ground. It spins out in fat drops, like a lather of amole. They make a loud noise when they run; they make a great din, as if stones were raining on the earth. Then the ground is pitted and scarred where they set down their hooves. It opens wherever their hooves touch it." The Mexica chroniclers also described black-skinned men with kinky hair, a reference to black and mulatto African-Cuban slaves who accompanied the Spaniards to Mexico. **The spies:** Mexica spies (*quimichtin,* literally meaning mice) were sent into foreign territories dressed as the locals and speaking their language. The spies carefully watched fortifications, barricades, movements of warriors, and military preparations. They paid dissidents in the enemy territories for information that, along with maps drawn by the spies, were sent back to the Mexica capital. **heads are enveloped in light:** halos.

The world is flat

These strangers pour fire into the craters of the moon.

On their hands, a strange poison glistens,
like the sickness of a devil.

These aliens steal sunlight and take the rain;
they hoard rainbows:
Their hearts are fragments of blackened jade,
jagged jade.

The foreigners finger gold disks like monkeys
and hastily bury topaz and obsidian in their souls.

They kneel before glittering mountains.
They weep before their agonized deity,
yet they still hunger for gold,
and their metal drips with blood.

A widening shadow crawls across México.

There is nothing to be resolved,
nothing returned.

What is done, cannot be undone.
Who is dead, is dead.

The world is flat;
everything that nears the edge falls off.

These strangers: Hernán Cortés and the Spanish conquistadores, who first arrived in México 1519. **their agonized deity:** the crucified Jesus Christ, depicted on the Roman Catholic crucifix, the indispensable symbol of Spanish Catholicism.

Malinalli

The cranes squawk in ancient tongues
as they lift towards the flattening sun.

The faces of the dead cast their ugly charm
across the sunset at Potonchán.

The Maya kings, disembodied,
hold court still in another world.
Their peace and fury rattle in the moonlight
from Xascabcheb to Uxkakaltok.

Malinalli, anointed with humid blue rain,
is sold for chalchihuitl stones and long tubes of incense.

She breaks sharp words,
like green and purple ears of maize,
into bowls of fantasy submerged
in the deepest, shadowy seas.

She keeps her thoughts smoldering in her heart,
like smoky fire.

Only the wandering lights in the night sky console her.

Potonchán: a village, now disappeared, in Mayan territory where Malinalli, a daughter of Mexica noblility, was sold into slavery. A Maya chief later presented Malinalli to Hernán Cortés as a concubine. Please see the poem, "La Malinche." **Xascabcheb to Uxkakaltok:** towns in Maya territory whose names have never been Hispanicized. **chalchihuitl stones:** jade stones. **tubes of incense:** containers of copal incense.

La Malinche

La Malinche is not flesh and bone,
but wind and rain.

She is spectral and transcendent,
living in our company,
and suffering from it.

We have crowned her La Chingada,
Our Lady of Thorns,
our queen of dismal days.

Our barbed tongues have lacerated her memory;
we have dismembered fact
and made men credulous to myth.

We have reconstructed La Malinche:
hammered her tremulous soul from the body,
and painted her face in solemn azure.

Men will never know her.

The hobgoblin fates cannot touch her.

She is remote and inscrutable, like time.

La Malinche, queen, lover of fatality,
preserver of México,
child of fertility and peace,
bender of souls.

La Malinche, who is of great beauty.

La Malinche: daughter of Mexica noblility, born *c.*1500 on the Isthmus of Tehuantepec. Her native name was Malinalli (or, Malintzin), which was the name of the twelfth day on the Mexica calendar meaning Grass, but also signifying bad luck and strife. Around 1510, Malinalli was sold into slavery among the Chontal Maya at Potonchán, a now-extinct village that was once located on the banks of the Grijalva River, probably near the present-day town of Frontera. She was presented to Hernán Cortés by a Maya chieftain in 1519 and became Cortés's interpreter, advisor, and lover, who played a crucial role in the conquistador's success in Mexico. Cortés himself called her *mi lengua*—my tongue. A Spanish chronicler described her as "outgoing, beautiful, and bothersome." The Spaniards baptized her "La Marina" or "Doña Marina"—She Who Comes from the Sea. But her own people would call her "La Malinche"—the traitress to the Indians—she who betrayed the Mexica nation. For hundreds of years, she has been stigmatized as a deceitful, unscrupulous, seductive woman. La Malinche has been portrayed as a quintessential symbol of betrayal. She is also called in Mexico—even now—La Chingada (the Whore, or the Skank). Rejecting that very negative depiction, Latina feminists celebrate La Malinche as a strong, vibrant, intelligent, and charismatic woman. In truth, La Malinche was a brilliant linguist who was fluent in Náhuatl, Yucatec, a Mayan dialect, and Spanish. Those who are sympathetic to La Malinche argue that she has been wrongly blamed for the Conquest of Mexico. It has been argued that La Malinche dissuaded the Spaniards from launching a full-blown military campaign that would have slaughtered thousands of natives. She has also been depicted—rather accurately—as the spiritual mother of the mestizos of Mexico as she, perhaps, gave birth to the first mixed-race Mexican child. "La Malinche's passivity is abject," the Mexican poet Octavio Paz wrote. "She does not resist violence, but is an inert heap of bones, blood, and dust. . . This passivity, open to the world, causes her to lose her identity; she is la Chingada. She loses her name; she is no one; she disappears into nothingness; she is nothingness." In one small sense, Paz was right. Little is known of La Malinche, who vanished from history in 1528, when the last reference to her appeared in Spanish colonial records of Temystitan-Mexico. In a very profound sense, however, Paz was wrong: for the life and legacy of La Malinche are still very much the source of historical debate among Mexicans.

A heart washed in chiles

The old moon faces Cholula.

    Stone idols swirl in a wash of stars.

The shadows of dead kings break across the heavens.

Hernán Cortés orders his men, and their iron,
into the proud city of Cholula.

Birds drop from the skies
and the expanse of years is compressed into a heartbeat.

The temples of the gods swim in seas of smoke
as the hundred lords of Cholula grimace a final time.
Their earth empties of song and breath.

Horses' eyes turn red in the flashes of gunpowder
that bathe the holy city in sorrow.

How will this barbarity be judged at the end of time?

Jaguars gather hungrily in the netherworld
and wait for their chalky prey.

Cholula: a sacred city, home to many shrines and temples and a bustling trading center. Cholula is one of the few Mexican cities with a record of continuous habitation from antiquity to the arrival of the Spaniards. Quetzalcóatl was the patron deity of the holy city of Cholula, whose citizens worshiped the cult of the plumed serpent, honoring the god for his benevolence and wisdom. The Cholulans constructed 365 temples inside their city—one shrine for each day of the year. Many of the magnificent stone structures were erected by foreign rulers so that their patron deities might bathe in the resplendent glow of Quetzalcóatl's aura. Believing that Quetzalcóatl had founded their city, the Cholulans established a towering pyramid for the feathered snake. The structure, the largest in pre-Columbian America, was called Tlachiualtepec ("the Mountain Made by Men"), originated in A.D. 180, when its innermost terraces had been laid. Pilgrims from as far as three hundred miles flocked to Quetzalcóatl's shrine at Cholula. The Spaniards later built the Church of the Virgen de los Remedios on top of the pyramid, whose sides, over time, have disintegrated. Because of its significance as a religious center, Cholula attracted immense flocks of pilgrims and ceaseless caravans of merchants so that the city was a haven for priests and tradespeople, not warriors and warlords.

In Tenochtitlán, Quetzalcóatl was revered, but that reverence was overshadowed by the worship of the Mexica population demanded by the deities Huitzilopochtli, Tezcatlipoca, Tláloc, and Cihuacóatl. Still, the Mexica royal mat (or, throne) was believed originally to be Quetzalcóatl's and would have to be relinquished to the god upon his return from exile. Please see the poem, "The serpent with brilliant feathers." In one sense, even if only on a symbolic level, Mexica kings boasted a direct lineage to Quetzalcóatl. Before taking the throne, Motecuhzoma Xocoyotzin was a student of theology, who had spent considerable time at the holy city of Cholula. There, Motecuhzoma cultivated a deep and abiding reverence for the creator god Quetzalcóatl, who was a relatively minor deity in the Mexica capital, but the paramount god for the Cholulans. As king, Motecuhzoma regularly examined oracles delivered to him by the vicars of Quetzalcóatl, the fasting priests in Tehuacan. Motecuhzoma raised Quetzalcóatl to a revered place inside the Mexica pantheon. **A heart washed in chiles:** Upon hearing of the massacre at Cholula (the subject of this poem), the Mexica great speaker Motecuhzoma Xocoyotzin said: "My heart burns, as if it has been washed in chiles." **The shadows of dead kings:** Mexica kings. **Hernán Cortés:** (1485-1547) Spanish conquistador; led the conquest of the Mexica empire, 1519-1521. **The lords of Cholula grimace a final time:** Having heard that the inhabitants of the ancient holy city of Cholula were planning to ambush his army, Cortés ordered many of the lords (the political leaders) of Cholula to be executed inside the Temple of Quetzalcóatl in October 1519. **Horses' eyes turn red:** The Spaniards and their Tlaxcalteca allies massacred between 3,000 to 6,000 Cholulan inhabitants. **Jaguars gather hungrily in the netherworld:** the Mexica understood that wickedness was punished by divine fury visited upon mortals by rains of fire, hurricanes, deluges, and vigilante jaguars, who tore into wicked people, eating their flesh. Next to snakes, jaguars were the most commonly carved animals by Mexica sculptors, thus reflecting how the imposing jaguar dominated Mexica thought. **chalky prey:** Mexica chroniclers observed that the Spanish conquistadores had faces as white as chalk.

The astronomers among us

Quetzalcóatl sets on fire the infant stars that burn over the temples, painted tombs, and the houses of turquoise.

His scriptures are written in the stars.

Always at sunset, the rapturous birds swirl around the sacred head of Quetzalcóatl, who flings fragments of stars
from one corner of the night sky to another.

The plumed serpent sings in the ears of the astronomers, who study the murky sky spotted with lights
to announce the time of obligation.

The astronomers track the bodies of heaven, fluid, shapeless, unconnected,
and make them cohere in the painted books.

A perilous, poisonous sunset

Quetzalcóatl, lord across the resplendent heavens,
who cajoled light to dance freely on the face of the young earth,
danced with that first sunburst,
weeping unabashedly before his gathered creatures.

Will mortals prosper in his refracted light,
that which burns fitfully before it is spent forever?

Or must they be consumed by monsters,
fading in a perilous, poisonous sunset?

Quetzalcóatl: (pronounced: Keht-sahl-coh'-atl) Mexica creator deity. **consumed by monsters:** the Mexica god Xolotl (who took the form of a skeleton with the head of a dog) was associated with monsters as was Tlalchitonatiuh, the earth monster.

The passion of Hernán Cortés

The young man's passion is sugar sweet,
a translucent moonlight. The words dance out of his heart
like a rhapsody.

A halo of birds encircles his head.

But his life is poured out, like water, on the earth.
And what was once sweet,
is sweet no longer.

The conquistador's passion is blood red,
congealed to dried blood.
His words are pinned to the heart of a monster.

The conqueror burns poems, kills songs.

Why, Hernán, why?

You dance as fire blooms from the cannons
and laugh as you shoot the exotic birds
as they whistle and sing in the aviaries.

Watch yourself, Hernán,
the earth beneath your feet is getting very hot.

Your own people will cut you to pieces,
and, having opened you,
will find the hurricanes and Indians you devoured.

In death, your eyes become frozen fire.

And your heart, still at last,
cut out of the body,
darkens eternally.

Hernán Cortés: The Mexica capital fell to an army of Spanish conquistadores and native warriors led by Hernán Cortés in 1521.

Tenochtitlán, under a clearing of stars

*The Spaniards suffer a plague of the heart
for which gold is a specific remedy.*
    ★ HERNÁN CORTÉS

Hernán Cortés plucks the black petals of iron in the dull dusk,
piling shadows and rusted rainbows
deep in the midnight.

His soldiers have taken the shining metals, moons, and soft winds,
leaving only a single cactus blooming in the night.

Tenochtitlán, under a clearing of stars. . .

Birds and fruit blown black in the first hours of night.
Half the lights fall dark in the city;
others have dimmed.

Soothsayers find no birds singing in the sacred places
and no light carved from cloud.

Quetzalcóatl put up the stars.
Quetzalcóatl pulls them down.

Fragments of stars float like dead frogs in the canals.

Hernán Cortés: (1485-1547) Spanish conqueror of México. **Tenochtitlán:** (pronounced: tay-noch-tee-TLAHN) capital of Mexica empire; present-day site of Mexico City. **in the canals:** the Mexica capital boasted a series of canals.

The stars are strange things

Quetzalcóatl weeps at his reflection in the looking glass.

Shadow precedes sun.

Light becomes a knot.

Motecuhzoma Xocoyotzin sees a setting sun in a jaguar's eye:
He reads the darkness in the twilight;
bonfires burn across the moon.
And the heavy clouds of autumn enter his bones.

Motecuhzoma sees his empire
burn in the cold and rain,
destruction blooming like maguey unfolding in the starlight. . .

The stars are strange things—
like divinities weeping over a dying people.

A fallen empire is beautiful washed in the light of the stars.

Quetzalcóatl: (pronounced: Keht-sahl-coh'-atl) The plumed (or feathered) serpent god. He was the giver of life, the inventor of time and writing, and the bearer of corn. According to Mexica religion, the demons of the underworld, jealous of Quetzalcóatl, gave him a mirror. The plumed serpent god was stunned to see his own reflection in the glass, which showed that he had a human face. He fled to the east on a raft of serpents, promising to return one day to judge the actions of men. Please see the poem "The serpent with brilliant feathers" for a more comprehensive discussion of Quetzalcóatl. **Motecuhzoma Xocoyotzin:** (pronounced: Maw-tay-kwah-SOH-mah Shoh-koh-yoh-tzin) (*c.*1468-1520) Mexica great speaker, 1502-1520; overthrown by Spanish conquistadores led by Hernán Cortés. The name Motecuhzoma means "Angry Like a Lord." The name Xocoyotzin signifies "Honored Young One." **maguey:** a cactus plant.

Cuitláhuac, dying on jade blocks

Cuitláhuac urges no welcome given
to the wolves at the gates:
>*I pray to our gods that you will not*
let these strangers into your house.
They will cast you out of it and overthrow your rule.

Clouds appear on the water;
eagles scatter in the late afternoon;
the gods have hidden their faces.

The sun becomes a fist of fire:
Ten thousand fires are open to the eastward.
Light is plucked from every city.

Cuitláhuac will become an empty hand,
a leaf blown across the earth,
a tree without shadow.

This year two eclipses will flourish across the skies.
The three towers burn from morning to evening;
the wolves are already in the city.

Cuitláhuac is dying on jade blocks;
the moonlight does not reach through his eyes.

This time tomorrow, his face become stone,
his voice heard only in dream.

Cuitláhuac: (prounced: Kwet-lä'wäk) (1470?-1520) Mexica great speaker. His name means "Owner of Dung." Human excrement was a valuable commodity in the manu-facturing of salt and in the curing of animal skins. Cuitláhuac was the son of Axayácatl and brother of Motecuhzoma Xocoytzin. **wolves at the gates:** Hernán Cortés and the Spanish conquistadores. **This year two eclipses will flourish across the skies:** a ref-erence to the deaths of two Mexica kings in 1520: Motecuhzoma Xocoyotzin and Cuitláhuac. **Cuitláhuac is dying on jade blocks:** Cuitláhuac contracted smallpox from the Spanish invaders; he died after a reign of only four months.

Cuauhtémoc hangs from the cruelest tree

The last king will die tomorrow,
so you hear the cranes crying ceaselessly
in the waterways.

The aliens with chalky and bearded faces
have already slaughtered the moonlight.

Every star in the blue and black sky is dripping fire,
burning our hearts, turning our hearts to smoke.

Into the prism, the colors of this world are caught, encased,
eternally bonded to stone.

Who will mourn the death of moons,
the extinction of our language?

Tenochtitlán is a smoldering twilight,
a beauty forever fading. . .

Cuauhtémoc hangs from the cruelest tree: The Mexica empire fell as Hernán Cortés ordered Cuauhtémoc (pronounced: Kwou-tem'ok) (1495?-1525) last great speaker of the Mexica, 1520-1525, hanged from a tree in 1525, following charges, probably fabricated by the Spaniards, that the Mexica king had been plotting to assassinate Cortés. Cuauhtémoc's name means "Falling Eagle." He was the cousin of Cuitláhuac and Motecuhzoma Xocoyotzin's nephew. **The aliens with chalky and bearded faces:** Spanish conquistadores.

The day of lamentation and remembrance

For a long while we have been menaced by the sky showing strange signs,
like those smoking stones
whose vapors illuminated the sky.

Once a ghostly light flashed, momentarily,
over the houses and the surface of the earth.

Now birds, pierced by arrows and pellets,
are falling to the earth.

Have these been presages announcing the strangers amongst us now?

These foreigners speak a barbarous tongue.
Everything they say is in a barbarous tongue.
It is as if they babble. What they say is gibberish.

These aliens conceal themselves and shoot brave warriors at a distance.
They do not cherish the scent of flowers. They do not paint poems.
Their bodies are swollen with avarice.
What are they but monkeys?

And they have gained many things in their hands.
We have only the grief in our hearts.

Our gods have fled across the sky, like clouds.
Our temples and shrines are fallen down.

Those spotted bodies, those bundles of shrouded and bound bodies, are precious green stones and flowers forsaken in the warrenous streets.

The world is turning upside down
as it does in a fit of vertigo:

We have lost our city.

We have lost our inheritance.

We have lost our way.

---

smoking stones: meteors. **Once a ghostly light flashed:** a zodiacal light that flared in the Valley of Mexico in 1509 (the Mexica year 4-House). A zodiacal light is a luminous tract in the sky seen in the west after sunset or in the east before sunrise and believed to be the light refracted from a cloud of meteoric matter revolving around the sun. "For many nights," recorded the historian Fernando de Alva Ixtilxóchitl, "there appeared a great brightness that rose from the eastern horizon and reached the heavens; it was shaped like a pyramid, and it flamed." **birds, pierced by arrows and pellets, are falling to the earth:** signs of the arrival of war. **presages:** presentiments or forebodings; prophetic impressions; something that portends or foreshadows a future event. **the strangers amongst us now:** Spanish conquistadors. **These foreigners speak a barbarous tongue:** The Mexica saw themselves as civilized, and the Spaniards as the barbarians and heathens. The Mexica scribes added: "They were like one who speaks a barbarous tongue. Everything they said was in a barbarous tongue." "It was as if they babbled. What they said was gibberish." These statements—and there are many more like them—clearly show that the Mexica did not see these newcomers as divinities—as gods walking upon the earth. **These aliens conceal themselves and shoot brave warriors at a distance:** Mexica methods of war emphasized the observation of pre-battle ceremonies that eliminated the possibility of surprise attacks. To the Mexica, battle was ideally a sacred duel between matched warriors. In fact, before the Mexica waged war on a town or province, they would often send arms to their enemies, to make sure that the contenders were evenly matched. However, the level playing field (if it can be described as that) meant nothing to the Spaniards, who shot their weapons at a distance. Whenever possible, the Spanish conquistadores avoided hand-to-hand combat with native braves and the Spaniards took refuge behind their cannons. The Spanish army targeted non-combatants and starved entire populations. The conquistadores employed horrific displays of public violence—as occurred at Cholula and Tenochtitlán. The Mexica saw Spanish soldiers as contemptible cowards. **Their bodies are swollen with avarice. What are they but monkeys?:** The Mexica were amazed by their first sightings of the Spaniards—with their weapons and horses. However, the Mexica did not revere the Spaniards as gods. The Mexica were stunned by the reaction of the Spaniards to the gifts of gold and precious feathers that were offered to them. A Mexica scribe wrote: "[The foreigners] picked up the gold and fingered it like monkeys. Their bodies swelled with greed and their hunger was ravenous; they hungered like pigs for that gold. They snatched at the golden banners, waved them from side to side and examined every inch of them." In this description, the Spaniards are portrayed not as divine, but as bestial—animal-like—and not superhuman, but sub-human. The Mexica analogized the Spaniards to monkeys and pigs. In the view of the Mexica, the Spaniards were different—repugnantly different. **Those spotted bodies, those bundles of shrouded and bound bodies:** victims of infectious diseases, especially smallpox. **precious green stones:** jade. **our city:** Tenochtitlán, the Mexica capital. **warrenous streets:** crowded streets. **The world is turning upside down as it does in a fit of vertigo:** from a Mexica description of the arrival of the Spanish army. **We have lost our inheritance:** a common sentiment among Mexica poets following the Spanish conquest of the Mexica capital.

Our former kings pray in dying light

Our dead kings sit in the quiet ether,
dethroned, snarling,
wounded jaguars bathed in blue, green light.

Their hearts are vessels of fire and ice,
drought and rain.

These former kings pray, haltingly,
in dying light and obsidian wind.

Who unravels the mysteries of life?

Not kings, for even they stand dumbfounded.

Our dead kings sit in the quiet ether: Upon his death, a Mexica king, wearing the brightly-colored mantles of the gods Huitzilopochtli, Tláloc, Xipe, and Quetzalcóatl, and a sumptuous black obsidian mask of the deity Tezcatlipoca, sat in state upon the royal *icpalli* mat, still ruling, for four days. Rulers and envoys from near and distant cities traveled to the Mexica capital to pay their respects to the dead monarch and offer him gifts to take with him to Mictlán, the kingdom of the dead. In addition, many of the king's slaves, jesters, musicians, and concubines were sacrificed, and their hearts cremated with the king's body so that they would accompany him on the long journey to the underworld. After his posthumous reign of four days, the king was cremated; his ashes were placed in a box and interred in an unmarked grave. Four years after his death, the king's most precious possessions and relics were buried, also without a marker. There was no cult of ancestors, or ancestor worship, in Mexica culture.

A luminous glow

¡Lumbre! ¡Tierra!

The dazzling Columbus, the Christ-bearer,
pulls la *Santa María* to shore under a brilliant sky
which not a single ominous cloud harasses.

From the decks of the three ships,
the wearied but still stunning Spaniards
cheer the navigator as he bows his head in prayer.

The Indians scramble in the morning sun,
stupefied by the fanfare of flags and crosses
and pale men embracing one another, and kissing the ground.

Columbus thanks his Father for these wretched souls to be saved
in this land where everything is green
and the singing of the birds is so sweet
that truly one would never leave this place.

Christoferens, the messenger of a new heaven,
preaches the Good News in these Indies
to a mostly naked throng,
to a people who have no idea what he is saying.

A few elders hum loudly as Columbus, the enlightened servant
of His almighty Savior, Christ, Son of Mary,
proclaims prophecies
as dark clouds roll in from the east.

¡Lumbre! ¡Tierra!: Spanish, "Light! Land!" This was the exclamation of a Spanish sailor upon the sighting of land, a few hours after midnight on October 12, 1492. It was a small island (Watling Island, now known as San Salvador Island) in the Bahamas. Columbus mistakenly believed that the Bahamas were islands lying off the Asian continent. **Columbus:** Christopher Columbus (1451-1506) Genoese navigator who led 120 Spaniards across the Atlantic Ocean in 1492. Columbus believed that he had reached the Indies, in Asia. Columbus made three subsequent transatlantic voyages. **the Christ-bearer:** Columbus's first name, Christopher, means the "Bearer of Christ." **la *Santa María*:** Columbus's flagship; named for the Blessed Virgin Mary. **Columbus. . .pulls la**

***Santa María* to shore under a brilliant sky:** this image is from Salvador Dalí's 1958-1959 dream-inspired painting, *The Discovery of America by Christopher Columbus.* **the three ships:** Columbus's three ships, la *Niña,* la *Pinta,* y la *Santa María.* **in this land where everything is green:** Upon landing in the Bahamas, Columbus wrote: "Everything is green and the vegetation is like that in Andalusia [in southern Spain] in April. The singing of the birds is so sweet that truly one would never leave this place." **Christoferens:** Towards the end of his life, Columbus signed his name "Xpoferens" (Christoferens), which means the "bearer of Christ." **the messenger of a new heaven:** Columbus viewed himself as a divinely anointed "messenger of a new heaven." He claimed that God had chosen him to bring the light of the New Testament to unevangelized regions of the world. **the Good News:** the New Testament. **the enlightened servant of His Almighty Savior, Christ, Son of Mary:** Above his new signature "Xpoferens," Columbus wrote the letters "X M Y." Some scholars have concluded that the cryptic letters signified: "Servant of His Almighty Savior, Christ, Son of Mary."

Indigenous spirits (or, the last testimony of Fray Bartolomé de las Casas)

We came from the Sea of Shadows,
with disease burning in our hearts.

All around us indigenous spirits have emerged
from shadowy seas of illusion
and will stare into our dumb, blank faces forever.

The flags of España snap in the wind,
the only audible sound
from the heart of Tenochtitlán
to Cuaba.

These indigenous spirits move across the New World,
dropping pearls into the mouth of fire.

The faces of the conquerors are consumed in smoke
and their silver turns to ash.

At last the stillness is broken
as jaguars hiss in the rising wind.

Fray Bartolomé de las Casas: (1474-1566) Spanish priest; condemned the enslavement of the native peoples of the New World. He wrote *Brevísima relación de la destrución de las Indias* [1552] and *Historia de las Indias* [first printed, 1875]. De las Casas was profoundly concerned about issues of sin and damnation. In his book *Apologética historia de las Indias,* de las Casas in part studied the designs of the Devil. **Sea of Shadows:** former name of the Atlantic Ocean. **España:** Spain. **Tenochtitlán:** (pronounced: tay-noch-tee-TLAHN) Capital of the Mexica empire. **Cuaba:** (also, Cubanacán) native name for Cuba.

Fray Bernardino de Sahagún quells the dispirited and rebellious ghosts

We Castilians are trapped by certain lights and shadows
fluttering over our heads unannounced,
like mean and pitiless spirits unleashed in the ether,
harassing our hearts and minds.

These tidings and happenings have been marked out
since the beginning of time.

And yet we are not completely imprisoned by the capricious fates.
The fates do not appear before us, like windblown plagues,
reigning as great kings.

A degree, or degrees, of latitudinarianism
turn us toward the good or the bad.

We have arrogantly proclaimed our refinement
and our righteousness,
while all the while falling freely
towards ignorance
and sin.

Have we already astounded the heavenly country of archangels and saints?

Castilians: inhabitants (in this case, conquistadores and friars) of Castile, a former kingdom, comprising most of Spain. **Fray Bernardino de Sahagún:** (1499-1590) Spanish Franciscan missionary and historian. After traveling to Mexico in 1521, Fray Sahagún learned Náhuatl so that he could interview the Mexica. Using detailed questionnaires, Sahagún collected oral and pictographic testimonies from Mexica authorities. He then critically compared their information and had it translated into Spanish. Sahagún compiled a twelve-volume encyclopedia (which took thirty years to complete) on every aspect of pre-Columbian Mexica life, including their beliefs and daily practices. In his encyclopedia entitled *La historia general de las cosas de Nueva España* (in English, *The General History of the Things of New Spain*), Sahagún strongly condemned human sacrifice and cannibalism as acts of evil. But he argued that there were many aspects of

Mexica culture that were worthy of admiration, including rigorous education and beautiful architecture. Sahagún wrote that Tenochtitlán was "another Venice." He praised Mexica songs, which he described as "very pleasing and even very mystical" and he celebrated Mexica poetic "excellences" and extolled their "marvelous language." Fray Sahagún argued that the Mexica used "very refined metaphors and admirable admonitions." **We have arrogantly proclaimed our refinement / and our righteousness, / while all the while falling freely / towards ignorance / and sin:** Fray Bernardino de Sahagún included a remarkable statement—a thinly-veiled rebuke of Spain—in his encyclopedia. "The Indians were so trampled and destroyed—they and all their things—," he observed, "that no sign remained of what they were before. And so they were considered barbarians and people of low degree. . .when truly. . .they are ahead of many other nations that are arrogant about their degree of refinement."

El no importa de España (A despot does not know his people)

A despot hoards light and peace.

Every weight and measure falls into his favor.

He has rain when he desires rain,
sun when he wants sun.

His precious birds sing only to him.

In his left hand, he holds jade,
in his right, golden artifacts.
All his greeds are satisfied.

A despot is an imposter,
parading as the man who knows things,
the blessed man, the clairvoyant,
who accurately marks time by sun and stars,
who proclaims himself the patron of life and death,
who makes straight the crooked places,
and reads every omen bathed in fog and smoke.

In truth, a despot knows nothing.

He speaks in vain,
for neither man nor animal hear him.
Still, he talks.

But his words become an ever-diminishing echo.

El no importa de España: Spain doesn't matter; from Francisco Santos' book, *El no importa de españa*, published in Madrid in 1668. **A despot:** a subtle reference to Hernán Cortés (1485-1547) Spanish conqueror of México.

The Nahua know what they know

The Nahua know what they know:

In their dreams they dreamed long ago,
they saw the two-headed deer
and the gods speaking in foreign tongues.

They knew all along that their temples
would be pulled down.

They knew all the while that the fire in the sun
would be blown out.

They knew all the while that the fire in the sun / would be blown out: an expression of Mexica fatalism.

The *Codex Vaticanus*

A red jaguar weeps on a hill hollowed out
and full of drooping stars.

A red jaguar: In Mexica theology, the jaguar was a deity in its own right. The jaguar-god was called Tepeyollotl, meaning "Heart of the Mountains." Tepeyollotl was the god of jaguars, earthquakes, and echoes. He was often portrayed as a jaguar leaping towards the sun. In the *Codex Vaticanus* (plate 19), a jaguar is depicted perched on a mountain hollowed and full of stars.

Nuestra Señora de Guadalupe and visions of a new kingdom in México

for His Holiness, Pope John Paul II

December 12, 1531.

Here is recounted, here is told:

Juan Diego Cuauhtlatoatzin hears the morning moon sigh a prayer
over the hilltop of Tepeyac, the Mexican Zion.

    Cranes fly enthralled in the frozen sky.

In the sun rising, Nuestra Señora, la Virgen de Guadalupe,
our Blessed Mother,
    Queen of the angels,
Queen of the prophets and apostles,
Queen of the martyrs,
appears in that sublime sunburst before Juan Diego.

She is clothed in turquoise mantle and maternity band.

This is the first favor, the first apparition,
the first image to originate in these lands.

Nuestra Señora de Guadalupe, the Light of Heaven,
offers the beloved Tonantzin, patron of gods and stars and ants,
the sign of the Son.

The Queen of Peace sends la paloma blanca
to soothe La Llorona sobbing along the riverbank.
Cu-cu-ro-cu-co paloma. . .

The golden-brown Virgin, She who comes from the moon,

brings hope and peace to the Mexicans, her holy children,
the new chosen people bending eternally
toward the heart of God.

Nuestra Señora de Guadalupe, La Purísima,
is enthroned in the rays of the sun.

She is enveloped in the light of the moon in the sacred heart of Metzico,
the New Israel, the New Chosen Land.

Laus Deo, et Virgini Guadalupensi
per infiniti saeculorum saecula.
Amen.

Here is recounted, here is told: In 1649, Father Luis Laslo de la Vega, vicar of tl sanctuary at Tepeyac, published a book entitled, *Huey Tlamahuiçoltica* (The Gre Happening) on the Virgin Mary's appearance before a native named Juan Diego. Tl work was published in Náhuatl (pronounced: NAH-wah-tl), the language of the Mexic One of the sections of the book begins with the words *Nican mopohua,* which mea "Here is recounted, here is told." This was a crucial section because it told in Náhu the story of the Miracle of Tepeyac, including dialogue between the Virgin and Ju Diego. This book played a crucial role in the veneration of Nuestra Señora Guadalupe as the protectress of the indigenous peoples. **Juan Diego. . .hilltop of 1 peyac. . .La Virgen de Guadalupe:** On December 12, 1531, Juan Diego, a poor nati and recent convert to Catholicism, heard sweet music not of birds, but of angels, a then he saw a young, brown-skinned woman radiant with light who informed him tl she was the Virgin Mary, Mother of the true God. The Blessed Virgin Mary appeared l fore Juan Diego on a hill called Tepeyac (or, Tepeyacac), near the village of Guadalup on the outskirts of Mexico City. The Blessed Mother told Juan Diego (whose nati name was Cuauhtlatoatzin, pronounced: Kwat-la-kwat-seen, and meaning "He W Talks Like an Eagle") (1474-1548) to go to the palace of the bishop of México, Juan Zumarraga, and tell him that she wanted a beautiful church constructed in her hon Juan Diego went to see the bishop, but His Eminence refused to believe Juan Dieg account.

Once again, the Blessed Virgin appeared before Juan Diego and again told him see the bishop. Once again, the bishop refused to believe the native. However, Zum: raga told Juan Diego that his story would be believed if he brought some sign that t woman he saw was the Blessed Mother. Juan Diego returned to Tepeyac, where he tc the Virgin of the bishop's request. Our Lady instructed the native to go to the top of t hill and gather flowers there as a sign. Juan walked up to the summit and found many roses blooming there in the midst of a freezing winter. He picked the roses and placed them in his tilma, or cloak. Our Lady told him to take the flowers to the bishop as the irrefutable sign.

Juan Diego returned to the palace and informed the bishop that he had brought a sign. He unfolded his tilma, and the roses came tumbling out. Zumarraga fell down to his knees in prayer. On Juan Diego's tilma was emblazoned an Image of the Blessed Virgin, exactly as she appeared to the native on the hill of Tepeyac. Work was immediately begun on a beautiful church for Our Lady of Guadalupe. **Tepeyac, the Mexican Zion:** Devotion to Nuestra Señora de Guadalupe intensified in the 1640s and 1650s. In 1648, Father Miguel Sánchez published a book entitled, *Imagen de la Virgen María, Madre de Dios de Guadalupe. Milagrosamente aparecida en la ciudad de México (Image of the Virgin Mary, Mother of God, Guadalupe, Miraculously Appeared in the City of Mexico).* Father Sánchez's book popularized the Miracle of Tepeyac among the Spaniards. During this period, Mexican Catholics were describing Tepeyac as a Mexican Zion and the divine image of Guadalupe was compared to the Ark of the Covenant. **Guadalupe:** an Arabic word meaning "river of wolves." This is an apt symbol for the Virgin who triumphs over demons and injustice. **turquoise mantle and maternity band:** When she appeared before Juan Diego, Our Lady of Guadalupe was wearing a maternity band around her waist, a sign of a mother about to give birth. She was also wearing a bluish-green mantle, or cloak. To the Mexica, the color turquoise was reserved for the great god Omecihuatl, a mother-father deity who was sometimes represented as a man, and other times as a woman. **This is the first favor, the first apparition, the first image to originate in these lands:** from Father Sánchez's book. Sánchez's actual phrasing was: "the first image to originate in this land." Here, the plural *lands* refer to all the Americas. **Tonantzin:** The appearance of Nuestra Señora took place just north from the old Mexica capital on the hill of Tepeyac. This was on the same hill where Mexica had worshiped Tonantzin, the mother of the gods, as "our venerated mother." Pilgrims from many places came to the hill of Tepeyac in an annual festival to worship Tonantzin, the gentle goddess. **patron of gods and stars and ants:** Mexican essayist and poet Octavio Paz celebrated the combined figure of Tonantzin and Guadalupe as the "mother of gods and men, of stars and ants." **la paloma blanca:** the white dove, symbol of peace. **La Llorona:** The Weeping Woman, in Mexica folklore. **She who comes from the moon:** Christ's traditional symbol is the sun, whereas Nuestra Señora de Guadalupe has been represented by the moon. The lunar symbolism is fitting as the Náhuatl name Metztli, the moon-deity, from which Mexico (pronounced "Mescico" by natives) means full moon, or "where the moon appears." **La Purísima:** The Pure One. **the Mexicans. . .the new chosen people. . .the sacred heart of Metzico, the New Israel, the New Chosen Land:** In his 1747 treatise *El Círculo del Amor,* Bartolomé Felipe Ita y Parra wrote that the Virgin Mary's miraculous apparition on Tepeyac hill had confirmed Mexico (or, in the native tongue, Metzico) as a new Holy

Land. "The Indian nation," Ita y Parra wrote, "eclipses and surpasses not only Israel but all the nations of the world." **Laus Deo, et Virgini Guadalupensi per infiniti saeculorum saecula:** Latin, Praise be to God, and the Virgin of Guadalupe, for ever and ever. Amen. These words venerating Nuestra Señora de Guadalupe reflect the institutional church's acceptance of the Miracle of Tepeyac. In the May 25,1754 papal bull *Non et equidem,* Pope Benedict XIV recognized Nuestra Señora de Guadalupe as the principal patron of New Spain (Mexico) and sanctioned the celebration of her feast day on December 12. On October 12, 1893, Mexican bishops crowned Nuestra Señora de Guadalupe as the eternal queen of Mexico. The elaborate coronation ceremony was conducted at Tepeyac. The Virgin of Guadalupe was praised and glorified as the foundress of the mestizo nation, since she had reconciled and united the natives and Spaniards in common devotion and faith.

Today, images of la mestiza María are ubiquitous in Mexico and in Mexican-American barrios (or, neighborhoods) in the United States. Images of the Virgin can be found in churches, in homes, in schools, in beautiful murals on the walls of buildings. During the 1965 grape strike in Delano, California—and in subsequent Mexican-American farm workers' marches throughout the Southwest—her image on banners emboldened and united the farm workers. December 12 (called el Día de la Virgen de Guadalupe) is a day of great festivities throughout Mexico, and in Mexican-American barrios. It is a feast day to celebrate the Miracle of Tepeyac. Regarding the adoration of Mexicans for La Virgen, the Mexican essayist Luís Dumois wrote: "Our Lady of Guadalupe has accompanied [Mexicans] in war and peace, in joy and grief, in life and death. . . She has been invoked and sought by us in times of despair and destruction, in times of serenity and reconstruction, then and now, as She will be tomorrow. I know that I can be a perfect Catholic and still not believe in Her. But I don't see how anyone can consider herself or himself truly a Mexican without trusting in the Lady from Heaven, Nuestra Señora de Guadalupe." In 1999, Pope John Paul II proclaimed Nuestra Señora de Guadalupe the patron saint of the Americas. On July 31, 2002, the pontiff canonized Juan Diego, the first native person of the Americas to be elevated to Roman Catholic sainthood. The canonization ceremony—which was held in the Basilica of Nuestra Señora de Guadalupe in Mexico City—blended Spanish music played with guitars with Mexica music played with drums, flutes, and conch shells while Mexica dancers performed before the Holy Father.

Two cranes in a nest

Two cranes, kissed by the morning sun,
sing in a ceiba tree
planted in the days of our great-great grandmothers.

---

ceiba tree: a large silk-cotton tree native to Latin America, growing to an average of thirty meters, with a substantial trunk. The tree was both functional and spiritual for the native peoples. Canoes were constructed from ceiba wood and the silky white fiber was utilized for mantles. The tree itself was sacred, celebrated as the "tree of fire" because the wood was also used to make fire-producing implements.

A supposed dream of St. Anthony's

I am alive!
I am no longer *persona non grata*.
I am the fire pawing at your eyes.
I am Vasco Nuñez de Balboa
     in a new found land.
          I am Balboa,
     kissing the lips of water;
          I am he,
     come here with my Cross and flag held high.

     I will be elevated, by grinning kings, in sight of God,
          and made to leap,
          choreographed
          in the great festival of souls.

     I am healed
     by cure of sun;

          I will live well.
I will pioneer with warriors and kinsmen
          across moon-lit straits,
     thigh-deep in passion:
discovering, at last, authentic fire
          dancing!
circling the perimeter of the still plantation.

Vasco Nuñez de Balboa: (1475-1517) Spanish explorer; crossed Panamanian isthmus to the Pacific, in 1513.

The spirits of cactus flowers

The spirits of cactus flowers
raise their porcupine heads
in our dreams.

In our dreams,
we have all the prickly flowers,
barbed fruit,
and the kings who wear thorny crowns.

We do not dream of Cíbola,
nor do we wish
for a pathway paved with topaz.

We have never coveted the hacienda on the hill.

Our bony prophets prepare our gift horses—
our fortune of knotted memories, sour yucca, dark moon.
A treasure buried in the sunset,
hidden from thieves.

The spirits of cactus flowers
plant a stark rainbow in our souls.

In our souls, a strange peace thrives.

Peeled starlight ripens only in our hands.

Cíbola: (pronounced: See'-bo-lah) is believed to be the original Zuñi native name for a group of pueblos or tribal lands in present-day Arizona. Believing that the area was rich in gold, the Spanish conquistador Francisco Vásquez de Coronado (*c*.1516-1554) led an army into the present-day U.S. Southwest in 1540-1541 to conquer Cíbola. The Spaniards found no golden artifacts there. **hacienda:** a landed estate.

Los espíritus de las flores de nopal

Los espíritus de las flores de nopal
levantan sus cabezas de espinas
en nuestros sueños.

En nuestros sueños,
tenemos nuestras flores espinosas,
frutas espinosas,
y los reyes que llevan coronas de espinas.

Nosotros no soñamos de Cíbola,
ni deseamos
un camino pavimentado de topacio.

Nosotros nunca hemos codiciado de la hacienda en la loma.

Nuestros huesudos profetas preparan nuestros caballos de regalados—
nuestra fortuna de memorias nudosas, yuca ácida, luna oscura.
Un tesoro enterrado en la puesta del sol,
escondido de los ladrones.

Los espíritus de las flores de nopal
plantan un arco iris rígido en nuestras almas.

En nuestras almas, una paz extraña prospera.

La luz de estrella pelada madura solo en nuestras manos.

Narváez

Anno Domini 1528.

Pánfilo de Narváez says the moon is made of gold.
He kneels before golden altars
as his heart hardens to ice.

Narváez sees a kingdom of gold swimming in the sea
north of Cuba.
     He swears he sees a golden sun
kissing La Florida.
         He traces a vein of gold in the earth.

Narváez brings a prism of somber colors
and the days become a rain of dying stars.

The cranes fly beyond the dark clouds,
fading against the sunset.

The earth goes still to Pánuco.

At La Española, moonlight bleeds to hurricane.

A chill wind blows across the three seas of La Florida.

The Spaniards crowd the gulf.
They cast their prayers to the wind.

No light, after the rain.

Narváez drowns in a sea of shadows.
His soul, like a stone dropped in the sea.

He makes no sound from the other side.

His lust for gold lodged forever in sea and shame.

Pánfilo de Narváez: (1478?-1528) Spanish conquistador and explorer. Narváez led an expedition to Florida in search of gold in 1528. He drowned in the Gulf of Mexico in the same year. **Pánuco:** in México. **La Española:** original name of the island of Hispaniola. **the three seas of La Florida:** the Atlantic Ocean, the Straits of Florida, and the Gulf of Mexico.

Pánfilo, adiós

Pánfilo de Narváez is stoic
as his ramshackle raft is taking on water.

He has no doubt that he is now heaven bound.

With a faint smile, Narváez says:
"I am as close to Mother Mary
by sea as by land."

Pánfilo de Narváez: (c.1480-1528) Spanish conquistador; led a 400-man expedition to conquer La Florida for Spain. The expedition was beleaguered by dwindling provisions, disease, difficult terrain, and native attacks. **ramshackle raft is taking on water:** Narváez and many of his soldiers drowned in the Gulf of Mexico when they attempted to return to Mexico aboard make-shift rafts. **Mother Mary:** the Blessed Virgin Mary.

Terrible wanderings

Álvar Nuñez Cabeza de Vaca and his companions shed their skins like snakes.

Their faces are sun-blistered, weathered by wind.

Their once strapping shoulders sag now,
their backs and breasts throb
under the cumbersome burdens they carry.

These haggard wanderers grub and eat roots, prickly pears
in the desolate wilderness.

They swelter in the sun and shiver in the wind.

They live but by the kindness of heathens.

These Spaniards are conquerors no longer,
neither in heart nor mind.

They are castaways dropped in a world
a million miles from Spain.

Álvar Nuñez Cabeza de Vaca: (*c.*1490-1557?) the treasurer of the Narváez expedition, and three other men were the only survivors of Narváez's attempt to conquer La Florida. Cabeza de Vaca and the others wandered in the American southwestern desert for nearly eight years before finding their way to Spanish settlements in Mexico. **Their faces are sun-blistered:** Exposed to the elements of sun, rain, wind, and cold, the Spaniards developed blisters and sores over their bodies. **These wanderers grub and eat roots:** The Spanish travelers survived on a diet of roots and prickly pears. **They live but by the kindness of heathens:** Cabeza de Vaca and the other Spaniards survived in large measure because of the generosity of the native peoples. **These Spaniards are conquerors no longer:** Having arrived in the "New World" as a conqueror and believing the indigenous peoples to be inferior to Europeans, Cabeza de Vaca developed a deep respect for native cultures and a contempt for Spain's abuse of them.

La Florida tristeza

Hernando de Soto has brought storm clouds over sierra,
a line of squalls over La Florida.

The shadows of dead kings pass over the everglades.

De Soto, conjurer of torrential hurricanes,
stone cactus,
tender of husked poison.

At his right hand: broken pottery, shattered pearls.

His image dances in the eyes of the devil.

Hyenas wail beneath a red copper moon.

La Florida tristeza: land of the rising specter,
hollow moon,
smoldering copal,
trampled palms, la porra.

La Porra, the living shadow.

Hernando de Soto: (*c*.1500-1542) Spanish conquistador and explorer. In 1539, De Soto began an expedition into what is now the southeastern United States. He died on the banks of the Mississippi River in May 1542. **La Florida tristeza:** sad Florida. **La porra:** The club.

The River of the Holy Spirit
(El Río del Espíritu Santo)

May 21, 1542

The moon hunches over the earth.
Her heavy wings droop across the dusk.

Dark clouds cross the waters.

The skies make no noise;
not even the crows make a sound.

Hernando de Soto runs his finger across the faces of the dead.

He calls out to the ghosts,
but there is no reply.

De Soto counts the ears of withered corn.

He closes his eyes and says a prayer under his breath.

El no importa de España.

Spain ends here.
There is nothing left of the Old World.
The New World withers in the conqueror's palms.

De Soto dies beneath a red copper moon.
He weeps as he dies: *"Forgive me, o Lord,*
for I have let evil take my hands."

But the hour of death is no time to cleanse the soul.

The River of the Holy Spirit (El Río del Espíritu Santo): Name given to the Mississippi River by the Hernando de Soto *entrada* (expedition). **May 21, 1542:** date of de Soto's death. ***El no importa de España:*** Spain doesn't matter; from Francisco Santos' book, *El no importa de españa,* published in Madrid in 1668.

La promesa

Among the prickly plants and mud flowers,
Francisco Vásquez de Coronado squints in the rising sun.

He is mesmerized by what he thinks he sees:
gleaming cities of gold boasting tall and jagged towers
rising gloriously towards open heavens.

El Gran Quivira, ten times more splendid than Tenochtitlán!

There is nothing that parallels this glory in Barcelona
or Sevilla.

In this cracked and gnarled desert kingdom,
Coronado's head fills with fantastic apparitions.

Everything appears gilded in the morning glow.

Oases flower in Coronado's tired eyes.

La promesa: The promise. **Quivira:** Inspired by native reports of a golden city called El Gran Quivira, Spanish conquistador Francisco Vásquez de Coronado (*c*.1516-1554) ordered his men to march from the Río Grande to what is now central Kansas in search of the splendid city. Coronado's expedition into what is now the southwestern United States spanned the years 1540-1542. **Tenochtitlán:** The spectacular capital city of the Mexica empire; conquered by Hernán Cortés's army in 1521.

La decepeción

The wild goose chase is over.
The dreams, the visions, the prayers, the sacrifices
yield nothing of the promise.

In the heart of Quivira,
Coronado and his conquistadores stand stupefied.

Stretching out before them yawn miles of cornhusks.

Maize, maize as far as the eye can see.
A kingdom of corn, and no trace of gold.

This is a disappointment as cold and bitter as death.

La decepeción: Spanish, The Disappointment. Please see previous poem for background information. Coronado's army arrived in Quivira only to find a tremendous amount of corn, but no gold. **maize:** corn.

Alta California

Even amid the scurvy and seasickness,
Sebastián Vizcaíno spins poems about this isla de Calafía, la reina.

In Vizcaíno's poems, seeds sprout blossoms,
birds chirp,
and the Blessed Virgin herself receives luminous petals
from the faithful.

Vizcaíno can read the future
in the golden corona around the sun:
he knows that men will call Alta California paradise
until the end of the earth itself.

What wealth shimmers in El Escorial
that this heaven on earth will pale by?

Sebastián Vizcaíno: (1550?-1616) Spanish explorer; commanded an exploratory expedition along the coast of Alta (Upper) California in 1602. Vizcaíno and his mariners entered San Diego Bay, Santa Barbara Channel, and Monterey Bay, reaching as far north as 43° North Latitude. **isla de Calafía, la reina:** Spanish, the island of Calafía, the queen. The Spanish name of California derives from an imaginary island in García Ordoñez de Montalvo's 1510 novel, *Las Serges de Esplandian*. The fictitious island was populated exclusively by women and ruled by a queen named Calafía. For many decades, the Spaniards believed that California was an island. **Vizcaíno's poems:** Vizcaíno's report on the coast of Alta California was so glowing in its praise that it is depicted here as poetry. **El Escorial:** an exquisite Roman Catholic monastery, located fifty kilometers northwest from Madrid, built by Spanish King Felipe II in the sixteenth century.

Cuatro de Septiembre de 1781

The friars raise a Crucifix in this land, open
save for rabbits and indigenous souls.

The king's colors are unfurled gloriously
following a chorus of hosannas to Nuestra Señora.

The Spaniards christen the new settlement
with the exalted name: El Pueblo de Nuestra Señora la Reina
de los Ángeles del Río de Porcíuncula.
The name rings like poetry, la escritura de Dios.

His Excellency, Felipe de Neve, prays that this pueblo shall forever
be Catholic and Spanish: "Seamos serios en nuestro trabajo
de modo que nuestra gente se multiplique aquí,
de que prospera la fe santa,
que la lengua materna nunca esté calmada en este lugar."

Padre Práxedes says Amen and now let the Indians come to us
and be blessed. Let the heathens rise from their lethargy
to kiss the feet of Our Savior, Christ himself.

Neve thrills at the coming days
when surely the Spaniards will be planted and prosperous here,
a praise and a glory,
una ciudad sobre una colina.

Cuatro de septiembre de 1781: September 4, 1781; the date of the Spanish founding of Los Angeles. **The friars:** members of Roman Catholic mendicant religious orders; in this case, Fransciscan priests. **El Pueblo de Nuestra Señora la Reina de los Ángeles del Río de Porcíuncula:** Spanish, The Town of Our Lady the Queen of the Angels by the River of the Little Portion; original Spanish name of Los Angeles. **la escritura de Dios:** the writing of God. **Felipe de Neve:** Spanish governor of Alta California. He personally selected the location for the founding of Los Angeles. **"Seamos serios en nuestro trabajo de modo que nuestra gente se multiplique aquí, de que prospera la**

fe santa, que la lengua materna nunca esté calmada en este lugar.": "Let us be earnest in our work so that our people multiply here, that the Holy Faith thrives, that the mother tongue never be stilled in this place." **una ciudad sobre una colina.:** a city upon a hill—an echo of the English Puritan view of sixteenth century Massachusetts Bay Colony.

This satellite of our blessed Zion refracts a holy light back unto our Lord

El Pueblo de Nuestra Señora la Reina de los Ángeles del Río de Porcíuncula, 1781.

Our antecedents, by all that they did,
have brought us into our plenty in this land.

We are more blessed than the Jews,
and nearly as sanctified as saints
as we build our homes and little ranches
in this land inhabited by the heathens.

We are prophets in both name and deed.
There is no light beyond the prophecies that we alone foretell.
This satellite of our blessed Zion
refracts a holy light back unto our Lord.

How will our own work and piety
be a praise and a glory to our distant descendants?

What will be said of us in twenty years' time? In two hundred years?
Will we be remembered in those strange and unknowable days?

Shall they who follow us, so many generations hence,
pray God that we first planted ourselves in this New World,
an ocean and a world from Spain?

El Pueblo de Nuestra Señora la Reina de los Ángeles del Río de Porcíuncula: Spanish, The Town of Our Lady the Queen of the Angels by the River of the Little Portion; original Spanish name of Los Angeles, California. **antecedents:** ancestors. **We are more blessed than the Jews:** a reference to the perspective that Jews, as descendants of the Israelites, are God's chosen people. **There is no light beyond the prophecies that we alone foretell:** an expression of Roman Catholic exceptionalism. **This satellite:** the Spanish settlement as a satellite of the Spanish government. **our blessed Zion:** Spain.

Lt. José Francisco Ortega's dispatch to the viceroy of Mexico

December 4, 1782

Your Excellency:

There is little of manmade quality
in this village and its environs,
for the heathens
have not done much here.

The friars have called the place *Santa Bárbara,*
for the saintly lady
who gave her life
so that she might have life.

The hamlet may now be desolate of citadel
and chapel,
but the lavender and colitis
and blue-green sea in this place
immure the manly heart
in solace.

In the times to come,
Spain will claim this town
as the finest jewel in its imperial scepter.

In the Names of Christ, Our Savior,
and His Majesty, King Carlos III,
I am yours obediently,

Lt. José Francisco Ortega.

Lt. José Franscisco Ortega: (1733-1798) born in Zelaya, Guanajuato Province, Mexico. He began his military service at Loreto, Baja California. He spent eighteen years in the service of the Spanish military, earning the rank of sergeant less than two years after his enlistment. Ortega took a brief leave from the military to serve as *alcalde* (or, mayor) of mining camps on the Baja California peninsula. After his return to the military, Ortega distinguished himself for his loyalty and work ethic, and was rewarded with the rank of lieutenant. Ortega served in the first Spanish land expedition to Alta California, commanded by Gaspar de Portolá in 1769. He was an accomplished explorer and superintendent of settlements: he may have been the first European to reconnoiter San Francisco Bay, served as comandante of the Presidio of San Diego, and helped to found the missions of San Juan Capistrano and San Buenaventura. In 1782, Lt. Ortega founded the Presidio of Santa Barbara. He was personally responsible for planning the fortifications and irrigation works and establishing orchards, farming, and livestock raising to sustain the presidio and Spanish settlement in Santa Barbara. Felipe de Goycoechea replaced Ortega as comandante at Santa Barbara in 1784. Ortega later commanded the presidio at Monterey and, briefly, at Loreto. In 1795, Lt. Ortega retired to Santa Barbara after forty years of military service to Spain. He died at his ranch at Refugio Beach in Santa Barbara on February 3, 1798, at the age of sixty-five. He was buried at the Mission of Santa Barbara. **the viceroy of Mexico:** Martin de Mayorga. **for the heathens:** the Chumash natives. **the saintly lady / who gave her life / so that she might have life:** In 1602, the Spanish explorer Sebastián Vizcaíno named Santa Barbara after St. Barbara, a third century seventeen-year-old martyred for her devout Christian faith. **Carlos III:** king of Spain, 1759-1788.

Santa Bárbara, 1784

Felipe de Goycoechea.

He was named, in 1784, to supervise
construction
of a permanent presidio
in SANTA BARBARA.

Goycoechea made friends with the Indians.

He bought fox skins from them.
He paid glass beads for fish.

He smoked pipes with them,
and bowed his head when their elders chanted.

He didn't see the Indians as riff-raff,
he didn't censure them,
as some Spaniards did after the first welcome.

Goycoechea hired the Indians,
paid them coin, corn,
beef jerky, and Puebla cloth
for their labor in building
El Presidio de Santa Bárbara.

The Indians gathered stone
from the mountains;
they made 20,000 adobe bricks of mud,
500 tiles were made from clay,
and the Presidio walls rose.

Indian sweat built the presidio.

Goycoechea raised his fists in the air
as the Fort was declared finished.

Felipe de Goycoechea: (also spelled, Goicoechea) born in 1747 in Cosalá, in Sinaloa, Nueva España (Mexico). Entering the military as a cadet in 1772, Goycoechea rose through the ranks quickly. He was named comandante of the Presidio of Santa Barbara in 1782, serving in that post until 1784. He later became governor of Baja California. Goycoechea died at Loerto, Baja California, in 1814.

Santa Bárbara, 1802

On Lt. Raimundo Carrillo / on kelp bass, barracuda, and leopard sharks;

on settlement: was it Catholicism,
or was it fish?

And, anyway, how will we ever know
now that tourism has won out over fishing.

> *The sea   The chill of the sea*
> *The primitiveness of the sea*
> *is beauty*
>
>   *The sea is beauty.*

1.

Raimundo Carrillo was born in Baja California in 1749,
and was raised a Catholic.
He loved the Church: its rituals, its tidings, its communion of saints.

He believed in the Holy Spirit, the Lord, the Giver of Life.

He acknowledged one baptism
for the forgiveness of sins.

2.

Carrillo, in his early twenties, came to Alta California,
served in the Army of the King of Spain,
and was first stationed at Monterey.

Unlike most military men, Carrillo preferred poems to guns,

    patience to gunpowder.

3.

He was made comandante of the Santa Bárbara Presidio in 1802
and, in that post, he served for five years.

Every day he sought the blessings of the priests,
he begged for wisdom in his decisions,
seeking the epiphanies only the blessed can know.

Carrillo treated the Indians with kindness.
          He gave them gifts, and when he spoke to them,
his words were as butter, not war.

And when Chief Yanonali died in 1805,
and was buried at the Mission,
Lt. Carrillo laid a toyon branch and tule bulrush
on the grave.

4.

Carrillo had no interest in "creaming" the Indians
or in pouring out his religion,
like water,
upon them.

He didn't destroy their localism,

he didn't shove the Indians aside.

———————

(José) Raimundo Carrillo: (1749-1809) born at Loreto, Baja California. Carrillo explored Alta California as a soldier in Gaspar de Portolá's expedition of 1769. Carrillo was comandante of the Presidio of Santa Barbara from 1802-1807 and then served as comandante of the Presidio of San Diego from 1807-1809. He died in 1809 and was buried in the chapel on Presidio Hill in San Diego.

Santa Bárbara, 1807

On José Darío Argüello / on the desire of adobes and agriculture;

on the consequences of taking what isn't yours,

on going out of bounds,

on how men use their lives:

1.

Argüello replaced Raimundo Carrillo
as Presidio comandante in 1807;
he gave thanks more than once for the covenant
that had brought the Spaniards such fish
and such natural beauty in Santa Bárbara
that language: the spoken word, and the written scripture,
become superfluous.

José Argüello gloried in his work

he loved work   he revered the ethic of work.

After the Earthquake of 1812 leveled the Presidio,
he picked up the pieces,
placed stone back upon stone.

> (Argüello wrote that it was presidio-making
> that he felt closest to, the adobe building,
> the gate keeping, the cattle raising,
> and shepherding of sheep, hogs, horses, and burros).

2.

Under Argüello, the Spaniards did not butcher the Chumash,
as the king's men had massacred the Mexica and Incas.

Argüello did not order the assassinations
of Chumash chiefs,

he never sent word that the sacred sites should be sacked,
the burial grounds desecrated.

The Indian villages along the coast were not torched.

3.

Argüello would have just as soon leave the Indians
alone in their localism,
he would've left them alone in their beauty,

but enough Spaniards believed they could always speak louder,
they could always own more,

so the Indians did get shoved aside.

José Darío Argüello: (*c*.1753-1828) born in Querétaro, Nueva España (Mexico) around 1853. As a young man, Argüello enlisted in the Mexican regiment of dragoons. Argüello participated in expeditions to the Colorado River and Los Angeles. In 1797, he was promoted to the rank of captain and was assigned as comandante of the Presidio of Santa Barbara from 1807-1815. Following the death of Governor José Joaquín de Arrilaga in 1814, José Darío Argüello also served as acting governor of Alta California, while he continued to live in Santa Barbara. The following year, he became governor of Baja California, serving in that office until 1822. He died in Guadalajara in 1828. Point Argüello located at Vandenberg Air Force Base in Santa Barbara County is named after him.

José de la Guerra's message
to the emperor of México

June 1, 1822

Your Worship, Agustín I, Emperor of México:

The messengers have brought Your Highness's reports into my hands.
The tidings they contain are boisterous tidings
heralding that Spain's grip on these provinces,
having been loosened, is now lost,
presumably forever.

I know the events of this hemisphere, and beyond,
must necessarily excite either felicitous or troubled passions,
but I study the times through a rose-hued lens;
all that I perceive and interpret
is perceived and interpreted
from my blessed exile in Santa Bárbara.

The world is surreally detached from me here,
although I feel strongly, as ever,
the burdens of my post.
And I am as scrupulous as ever I have been,
and I do what I can do.
Beyond that, I am only a bystander
as history is made and remade.

May the Savior, Christ Jesus, keep his hands on you and your regime:

Your obedient servant,

José Antonio de la Guerra y Noriega,
Comandante, Presidio de Santa Bárbara, Alta California

José Antonio de la Guerra y Noriega: (1779-1858) born in Novales, Spain; at thirteen years old, he emigrated to Mexico City to live with family members. De la Guerra joined the Spanish army in 1793 and was appointed a cadet in 1798 at the Presidio of San Diego. De la Guerra was named the acting comandante of the Presidio of Monterey in 1804, and two years later, was transferred as a lieutenant and comandante at the Presidio of Santa Barbara in 1827; he served in that post until 1842, when he retired to manage his vast half-million acre land holdings in Alta California. José de la Guerra died in Santa Barbara, California in 1858 and was buried at Mission Santa Barbara. **Agustín I, Emperor of México:** In 1821, following an eleven-year struggle against the Spanish mother country of King Fernando VII, Mexican insurgents, led by General Agustín de Iturbide (1783-1824), secured their national independence. Iturbide marched into Mexico City in September 1821, where he received the symbolic gold keys to the city. On May 18, 1822, Generalísimo Iturbide proclaimed himself emperor of Mexico, assuming the name Agustín I. The following day, the Mexican Congress, intimidated by the emperor's military resources and mobs that favored him, declared Iturbide the constitutional emperor of Mexico. He was officially crowned on July 21, 1822. Emperor Agustín I proclaimed before God that he would defend the Roman Catholic faith, which would be granted a monopoly on the spiritual life of the Mexican empire. Despite the pomp and pageantry of the new imperial Mexico, the nation was beset by a depressed economy and factionalism between monarchist and antimonarchist elements. Agustín abdicated his throne in February 1823 and Mexico was declared a republic.

You see it was always fishing

★ for Dr. Curtis Brian Solberg, teacher & friend

I.

It was fishing that was first
in the channel.
Even after the railroad came,
it was fishing.
And when this town was a cow town,
it was fishing.
Before this pueblo was on the map,
it was fishing.

How many generations of Indians
took the tomols offshore
in search of rockfish & swordfish,
cabezon, cod, and bonito,
abalone and octopus?
How many times did they feast on whale fat?

How many prayers were sung to the mother ocean?

II.

Then the Spaniards colonized the coast.
And it was fishing that survived Cabrillo
& Vizcaíno. It was fishing
that survived the missionaries & the visionaries.
In the end, it was fishermen who lived on
beyond the comandantes & soldados.
It was fishing that was first.
Even after the Presidio was raised,
stone upon stone,
& the adobes, too, of mud brick,

it remained fishing.
And the vaqueros came here, with their cattle.
But it remained fish.

The Spanish immigrants must have reveled
at the beauty of the shore
from, say, Mission Creek out along East Beach and out to sea
where the sun sets
behind the channel islands.

The padres must've seen Christ alive
in the fishing work:
as sea bass, jack-smelt, and perch
were caught in the channel
& brought back as sustenance
on the rancheros & the encomiendas.
You see it was always fishing:
it was always fish;
our history is men after fish.

III.

Three generations ago,
the Italian brothers Geobatta & Salvador Castagnola,
fished from skiffs in the kelp beds,
sold their catch to: Larco's Fish Market
at 214 State Street,
where a sign in the window sang:
FISHSELLER WILLING TO DELIVER.
The Larco family cleaned & canned fish
& shipped the treasures north to San Francisco
and south to San Pedro.
Sebastian Larco made a habit of giving thanks & praise
for his blessings before he'd take his steamer, the *Cuba,*
off the beaches of Goleta & Isla Vista
and drop the gill nets and seine nets
in thirty feet of water,
where Santa Barbara's Chinese fishermen
caught soupfin sharks. On Stearns' Wharf,

at sundown, the Chinese men cut off
the fins. The pectoral. And dorsal,
and dried 'em in the next day's sun,
The tanned fins were later stirred in soup.

IV.

Cody Machado and his brothers, Pokey and Kelly,
unload their father's day's catch on the Navy Pier, in the harbor.
A radio chirps. Two blond boys from Indio Muerto Street
poke sticks at the dead yellowtail.
A dog barks mindlessly at fish tumbling in the matted nets.

*

Smell of sea, smell of fish
& petroleum.
Smell of sweat & sea salt:

This is my home
until the Lord makes a sunset of my heart.

---

tomols: dugout canoes. **Cabrillo:** Joáo Rodrigues Cabrilho (Spanish, Juan Rodríguez Cabrillo (?-1543) Portuguese explorer in service of Spain; led first European expedition along California coast, 1542-1543. **Vizcaíno:** Sebastián Vizcaíno (1550?-1616) Spanish explorer; led expedition along California coast as far as 43° North latitude. Vizcaíno entered Santa Barbara channel on December 4, 1602. **comandantes & soldados:** commanders and soldiers. **Presidio:** the royal Spanish fort at Santa Barbara, founded in 1782, near the modern intersection of Cañón Perdido and Santa Barbara Streets, in Downtown Santa Barbara. **encomiendas:** estates. **vaqueros:** Mexican cowboys.

Un fútil pensamiento

para Mamita

¿Conoces tu madre,
la madre mar?
   ¿Conoces tú los misterios que esconde?

¿No les darás a estos misterios
más que un fútil pensamiento?

¿Conoces tu madre, / la madre mar?: Do you know your mother, the mother sea? **¿Conoces tú los misterios que esconde?:** Do you know the mysteries she hides? **¿No les darás a estos misterios / más que un fútil pensamiento?:** Have you ever given these mysteries a passing thought?

The last heartache of Manuel Crescion Rejón

Mexico City, May 25, 1848.

I have not consulted the palmist or those seers,
the self-proclaimed messiahs,
who look cryptically into the future.

Look how they swoon over their extravagant prophecies!

They are zealots whose eyes glow from some fire,
whose prophecies are nothing but smoke.

I have no need of clairvoyance,
for I draw upon the past as my map and muse.

And I see clearly what will come from this troublesome peace:
Our people, dispossessed of their motherland,
will live as aliens in the land of their ancestors.

How will they make sense of who they are,
where they are?

Who, for them, will be the guardians of memory?

The old habits, customs, song, dance, pastimes—
the very life of memory, its detail and meaning,
will vanish, degree by degree, like the sun at dusk.

The tribal markings will fade.

A people become faceless, rootless, soulless
if they have no connection to the past.

Where there is no transcendent memory and imagination,

there can be no tribal remembrance, no collective immortality.

What is lost from the predecessors will *never* be regained.

Our own people in the north have already lost their dead.
They do not feel the phantoms weighing upon them obscurely.

Whosoever they become,
they will not be the true heirs of the ancestors.
They will become something else,
enigmatic and eternally unknowable.
The mystery of regeneration will stop with them.

The bonds of consanguinity weaken
until they are no longer bonds.

The last heartache of Manuel Crescion Rejón: Mexican diplomat Manuel Crescion Rejón lamented the ratification if the Treaty of Guadalupe-Hidalgo, which ended the U.S.-Mexican war in 1848. Mexico lost nearly one-half of its territory to the United States in the treaty. Mexican diplomats, including Rejón, along with ordinary Mexican citizens expressed concern about the fate of Mexicans living in the "lost territory" now under U.S. jurisdiction. There were many unanswered questions at the end of the war regarding Mexicans living in the conquered lands, including issues of civil rights, land titles, language, religious freedom, and preservation of ancestral ways and culture.

As a result of these concerns, the preliminary draft of the Treaty of Guadalupe-Hidalgo included three crucial provisions—Articles VIII, IX, and X—regarding the rights of Mexicans in the so-called "conquered" territory (known as the "ceded land.") Article VIII specified that Mexicans in the ceded land had one year to choose whether to leave for Mexico or remain in the lands now under U.S. jurisdiction. There were approximately 80,000 Mexicans living in the ceded territory in 1848. About 2,000 chose to leave; but most remained on what they considered—rightly—to be *their* land, living in their established homes. Article IX of the treaty guaranteed that those Mexicans who remained in the ceded territory would enjoy all the rights of United States citizenship. They would enjoy all the liberties guaranteed by the U.S. Constitution. Their language and religion would be protected. Article X stipulated that all grants of land made by the Mexican government would be respected as valid by the U.S. government. Article X was absolutely crucial, because it would have protected the ancestral land titles of Mexican-Americans. However, the U.S. Senate refused to accept Article X. U.S. Senators worried that that provision would cause vexing problems for American landowners in Texas. The U.S. Senate deleted Article X from the final draft. Mexican President Manuel de la Peña y Peña and other Mexican officials strenuously protested the omission of Article X. Secretary of State James Buchanan informed the Mexican Foreign Relations Office that Article X was completely "unnecessary." According to Buchanan, Articles VIII and IX in the Treaty of Guadalupe-Hidalgo and the U.S. Constitution itself amply protected Mexican property rights. The Mexican Congress made statements that it would not ratify the Treaty of Guadalupe-Hidalgo without Article X. To assuage the consternation of Mexican officials, the U.S. government issued what it called the Statement of Protocol in May 1848.

The Statement of Protocol had two important provisions: 1. The American government—by suppressing Article X—did not in any way intend to annul the land grants of Mexican-Americans. 2. Mexican-Americans would be allowed to have their land titles acknowledged in U.S. courts. However, the American court proceedings were conducted in English, which most Mexican-American landowners did not understand. Additionally, Mexican-Americans were compelled to spend large amounts of money hiring Anglo lawyers to defend their land claims in U.S. courts. Mexican-Americans were now at the mercy of American courts, which frequently ruled against their land claims. With the Statement of Protocol having been issued, the Mexican Congress ratified the Treaty of Guadalupe-Hidalgo.

In practice, Articles VIII and IX in the treaty and the Statement of Protocol were simply ignored during the nineteenth and twentieth centuries. Article IX gave Mexican-Americans the right to retain their language. In *theory,* the U.S. government was compelled to publish its documents and conduct its business in both Spanish and English. And in *theory,* Spanish classrooms were to be provided for Spanish-speaking children. In *reality,* English quickly replaced Spanish as the dominant language in the Southwest. Mexican-Americans who did not understand English were at a decided disadvantage in many ways. Mexican-Americans were guaranteed freedom of religion—and most continued to worship as Catholics. However, Mexican-American Catholics in the Southwest were inundated by a flood of Anglo-American Protestants who held Catholicism in contempt. In reality, most Mexicans in the United States were considered a *class* and a *race* apart, separate and unequal, from the dominant Anglo-American culture.

In 1848, Rejón prophesied that Mexican-Americans would suffer great indignities in subsequent years. Only days after the Treaty of Guadalupe-Hidalgo was signed, Rejón commented: Our race—our unfortunate people—will have to wander in search of hospitality in a strange land, only to be ejected later. Descendants of the Indians that we are, the North Americans hate us, their spokesmen depreciate us, even if they recognize the justice of our cause. They consider us unworthy to form with them one nation and one society. They clearly manifest that their future expansion begins with the territory that they take from us. They push aside our citizens who inhabit the land." Rejón was right. Following 1848, Mexican-Americans encountered a host of indignities: the loss of property, segregation in public facilities (including schools), housing segregation, and poll taxes.

The United States profited enormously from the Mexican War: The U.S. acquired a massive amount of land (950,000 square miles) that was rich in farmlands. That territory had abundant natural resources, such as gold, silver, zinc, copper, and oil, which fueled the rapid industrialization of the United States. The United States also acquired ports on the Pacific that generated further economic expansion across the ocean. For Mexico, the loss of nearly one-half of its territory following the Mexican War had profoundly adverse effects. Mexico was left with shrunken resources. For the rest of the nineteenth century—and beyond—Mexico was severely hampered in its ability to build a proper economic infrastructure. Meantime, Mexico's population was growing rapidly. As a result—in the years to come—untold thousands of Mexican citizens migrated north, in search of economic opportunities inside the United States, especially in the Southwest, into a land of strangers, yet the very land of their ancestors. Please see the subsequent poems in this section. **May 25, 1848:** The Mexican Congress ratified the Treaty of Guadalupe-Hidalgo on that date. The United States Senate had ratified the treaty in March. U.S. President James Knox Polk declared the Treaty of Guadalupe-Hidalgo to be in effect on July 4, 1848. **Our own people in the north:** Mexicans living in the ceded territory. **The bonds of consanguinity:** the ties of kinship.

Henry David Thoreau ruminates on the recent war

As peace is of all goodness, so war is an emblem,
a hieroglyphic, of all misery.

★John Donne, "Sermons" [1622]

Every heart is divisible, either from dirt or stardust.

Take any one of our hearts as an emblem,
blurred, dusky, a twilight caught in microcosm.

Our heartstrings are drawn from scattering ash,
blown ash, blown polar white and cold.

Who among us held to a theology
higher than the vain deceits within our own hearts,
deceits gathered up like some strange language?

So we learned war in love of brass to gold,
in love of country, in loathing of cowardice.

We dispensed with philosophies and deliberation
as we burned down our neighbor's house.

And so that hieroglyphic, dark, immutable, is left,
a badge stamped on our hearts.

Henry David Thoreau: (1817-1862) U.S. poet, essayist, and Transcendentalist philosopher. Thoreau strenuously opposed the U.S.-Mexico War of 1846-1848. **we burned down our neighbor's house:** U.S. invasion of Mexico.

El procesión de los equinoccios

The border between the United States and Mexico stretches two thousand miles from the Gulf of Mexico to the Pacific Ocean. Poet Gloria Anzaldúa has described the border between the two countries as an open wound

★ UNA HERIDA ABIERTA

This border bleeds. This wound lives.
It sighs, sobs, sings.
It is tormented, yet sustained by sun.

These borderlands have no past to mark with fiesta
or solemnity.

To some, this frontier is a no man's land,
zone of fevered or frozen desolation.

But these lands are rich in ritual,
made majestic by moon and blood.

Here are holy lands, a thorny utopia,
a cursed blessedness,
where pilgrims have suffered, died, and were buried.

They have risen, like their God,
from sorrow to sanctity.

Along the length and breadth of this border,
the equinoxes come and go, like refugees,
faceless but full of faith.

El procesión de los equinoccios: The procession of the equinoxes.

In the shadows of the Apaches

The Apaches will give us no more trouble.

Their guns and horses and all their hocus pocus,
cannot help them now.

Today, the sun rises on the white man's country
and we will take
all that we can get.

Bring the Sonorans here to Tombstone and to Bisbee.
Bring them by the hundreds,
and by the thousands.

The Sonorans have silver in their blood.
The grim, grunt sounds of the mines
reverberate in their collective mind.

So send the starving Sonorans
down
in-
to the deep
arteries
of the earth.

God knows what ghosts they'll see through the dust and dirt
in the tunnels and pits
and who knows how many will be blown
to Kingdom come
by TNT that blows a bit too soon.

But I'm glad to say that the Mexicans
will bring up enough silver and copper
to make it all worth our while.

The Apaches will give us no more trouble: the "pacification" (a euphemism for the extermination and dispossession) of the Apache natives in the U.S. Southwest by the

U.S. Army in the 1880s opened new lands for whites to mine and otherwise develop. **Sonorans:** during the late nineteenth and early twentieth centuries, many impoverished Mexicans from the state of Sonora were recruited to work in the U.S. Southwest, particularly in the silver and copper mines in southern Arizona. **Tombstone. . .Bisbee:** mining communities in southern Arizona. In the late nineteenth century, a mining boom in the U.S. Southwest occurred, spurred on by the railroads and the need for copper in telegraph and electric lines. In 1880, California industrialists established the Copper Queen Mining Company in Bisbee, Arizona. At that same time, eastern business interests founded the Phelps Dodge Company, a major copper producer. Many Mexican-American residents in the Arizona and New Mexico territories, along with immigrants from the Mexican state of Sonora, worked in the Arizona copper and silver mines. The labor was arduous and dangerous, pay was low, and living conditions were abysmal. This poem describes the labor conditions of Mexican miners in the desert of Arizona, sometime in the 1880s or 1890s. **The Sonorans have silver in their blood:** the tradition of silver mining in Sonora dates back to 1640. **the dust and dirt in the tunnels and pits:** Mexicanos, and other miners, faced great hardships in the tunnels, pits, and smelters. Accidental dynamite explosions, machinery accidents, leaks of poisonous gasses, landslides, and stifling air were among the dangers that all miners routinely faced.

Reaching for utopia

Mexicanos are battered in the whirlwind.
They feel the devil sniping at their heels.

They flee, like roadrunners, across the border from Juárez.

Their hearts are soothed in the sunrise over El Paso.
But their peace is tenuous.
It sighs amid the barbs and taunts of los Americanos,
    who want them gone.
"There are enough greasers in South Texas."

So Mexicanos look for a new world in the west.
With horses and wagons they cross New Mexico
and Arizona. Some stay in Nogales.
Los deterrados bloom in the desert.

Men lay track for the Atchison, Topeka, and the Santa Fe.
They bend their backs on the Southern Pacific,
making their way to where the sunset ends.

Through Mexicali,
Mexicanos come.

Across the Salton Sea and Calexico,
these beautiful and handsome pilgrims enter the Golden State.

In East Los Angeles,
near the sacred roots of Calle Olvera
and La Placita,
Mexican immigrants plant a gorgeous new sun in the sky
and hear Nuestra Señora sing their names to her Son.

---

the whirlwind: the violence and dislocation of the Mexican Revolution (1911-1920), which drove thousands of Mexicans northward, into the United States. **Juárez:** Ciudad Juárez, in México. **El Paso:** in Texas. **greasers:** pejorative term for Mexicanos. **Nogales:** in Arizona. **Los deterrados:** The uprooted. **the Atchison, Topeka, and the Santa**

Fe. . .the Southern Pacific: Mexicanos worked on railroad construction in the American Southwest during the late nineteenth and early twentieth centuries. **where the sunset ends:** California. **Calle Olvera and La Placita:** site of the Spanish founding of Los Angeles in 1781, now in the Downtown district. **Nuestra Señora:** Our Lady of Guadalupe, the Blessed Virgin Mary.

God's imprint is on the hulled rice

March 12, 1875

In Los Angeles: there is clean water;
the voice of typhus is silent.
Dazzling birds sing in the marketplaces.

The sun nests over turquoise water.

Nuestra Señora de Guadalupe llenó la cornucopia
      y la gente tiene suficiente para comer:
suficiente torta de pascua
         y arroz con pollo.
Plenitud de grano.
Y plenitud de atún y bacalao.
Las trampas de pescado están llenas.
La gente tiene agua limpia.

Benevolence is at the flower and at the root. . .

God's imprint, not the government's, appears on the hulled rice.
The Lord giveth and the Lord taketh not away.

Corn, cattle, cotton, water, wheat.
The granaries are overflowing with the grace of God.

A consecration;
the people are consecrated;
      they are not wronged by their Father.

Shadows lift from roots and towering totems.

Ghosts thrive in the light of the shattered stars.

Nuestra Señora de Guadalupe llenó la cornucopia / y la gente tiene suficiente para comer: / suficiente torta de pascua / y arroz con pollo. / Plenitud de grano. / Y plenitud de atún y bacalao. / Las trampas de pescado están llenas. / La gente tiene agua limpia: Our Lady of Guadalupe fills the cornucopia / and the people have enough to eat: / enough Easter cake / and chicken with rice. / Plentiful grain. / And plentiful tuna and cod / The fish traps are full. / The people have clean water.

Sonoratown

Sunday, July 7, 1889

Sonoratown sparkles in the summer sun
as boys lift Nuestra Señora to the heavens.
A cavalcade of immigrants and clergy
flourishes along Calle Principal and across Eternidad.

Penitents walk barefoot on dirt streets
as the bells sing, perched in the towers of the old churches.

The fragrance of frijoles de la olla,
bowls of onion, cheese, chiles,
and steaming tortillas and tamales
swirl, delightfully, in the heart of barrio.

At night, garlands of colored lanterns glow,
candles flicker and fireworks sizzle,
as the blessed flock envelops the sacred heart of Jesus.

God himself has festooned the stars across his heavens.

Somewhere hidden above the crooked fences
and tidy ramshackle barrio,
the owls testify to this immense blessedness.

Sonoratown: name for the Mexicano barrio, centered on the old plaza, in the downtown district of Los Angeles, slightly west of the Los Angeles River. Many Mexican immigrants from the state of Sonora were residents of the area. **boys lift Nuestra Señora to the heavens:** an image of the Blessed Virgin Mary. **Calle Principal:** now Main Street, in Downtown Los Angeles. **Eternidad:** now called Broadway, in Los Angeles. **the old church:** in the Plaza district. **frijoles de la olla:** freshly cooked pinto or black beans from the pot. **tidy ramshackle:** an intentional oxymoron.

Cholo Hollow

1898 or 1899

Is this ground made blessed by locomotive oil
and steel track that lurches from here
to nowhere?

What redemption may be found in this desolation?

Here, at Cholo Hollow, these Mexicanos, rich in spirit,
construct altars from cardboard and corrugated tin.

They whisper hymns in the hope of salvation.

They sing prayers for loved ones
        who have already entered into the Kingdom of God.

Their faith flourishes from their bitter tears.

There is surely a holiness among the rusted track
and box cars. There is a blessedness in this poverty.

This is a sanctity that men, fat with riches,
do not know.

Cholo Hollow: a San Bernardino, California barrio that emerged in the 1890s in the
Santa Fe Railroad Company maintenance yards. Anglo-Americans referred to the colony
as Cholo Hollow.

Las siete palabras

Ventura, California, 1903.

The refugees, with callused hands
and frayed feet,
kneel in the sugar beet fields under the largest sky in the world.

On this holiest day of the year,
the migrants put aside their tools.

They cast away their handfuls of half-dollars.

They put away their grievances.

They lay their pain and their flowers beside the weeping Virgencita.

Las siete palabras: On Good Friday, Mexican Catholics commemorate Christ's last seven words: "Into your hands I commend my spirit." The solemn observation includes condolences offered to the Blessed Virgin Mary in a tradition known as El Pésame a la Virgen (The Sympathy, or Condolence, for the Virgin). **These refugees. . .kneel in the sugar beet fields:** Mexican migrant workers labored in sugar beet fields in Ventura, California at the turn of the twentieth century. In fact, the first significant strike of Mexican farm workers in the United States occurred in Ventura in 1903. **handfuls of half-dollars:** Mexican farm workers were sometimes paid in half-dollar coins.

The evils of necessity

There is no reason to whine about the flood of Mexicans
pouring into our country.

We need these poor folk here
who will work for next to nothing.

We need the greasers grubbing cactus and chaparral,
clearing land for cotton and carrots,
lettuce, spinach, and beets.

We need them tending tomatoes.

But the Mexicans can do so much more
than just plant and reap.

These greasers have a sorcerer's touch with silver.

At Bisbee and Tombstone,
they mesmerize metal;
they lure silver toward sunlight.

And these brown aliens nurse the locomotives
from Yuma to Topeka.

All this is menial work that Mexicans do best.

The wetbacks are the new niggers of America.

---

greasers: derisive name for Mexicans. **Bisbee and Tombstone:** mining communities in Arizona. **these brown aliens nurse the locomotives:** Mexican immigrants worked on Southern Pacific Railroad and Atchison, Topeka, and Santa Fe Railroad maintenance crews. **wetbacks:** pejorative for Mexicans. **new niggers of America:** an American entrepreneur commented at the turn of the twentieth century that Mexican immigrant workers were "a new class of niggers" in the United States.

The wonderful city of the magic motor

The motors whir rhythmically in the ears of Mexicans
as poverty spreads like a blight
across the villages of Sonora, Chihuahua, and Coahuila,
as an empty sun rises
over Nuevo Leon and Tamaulipas.

The black Tin Lizzies dance like sugarplums
in the dreams of los mexicanos.

It is so easy to up-
root the poor
from this broken country.

Each day, the railroads whisk away hundreds of campesinos
to the U.S. heartland.

Does Mexico ever weep over the loss of her strong and handsome young men?

The wonderful city of the magic motor: Detroit, Michigan. In the 1920s, young Mexican men, mainly from northern Mexican villages, were attracted to Detroit to work in Henry Ford's automobile factories. **Sonora, Chihuahua, Coahuila, . . . Nuevo Leon and Tamaulipas:** states in northern Mexico. **Tin Lizzies:** Ford Model-T automobiles which Mexican workers assembled in Detroit. **campesinos:** peasants.

Rafael frees himself from the past

November 2, 1923.

Somewhere off the Mexican coast,
the steamship belches a sea of black smoke
toward the rising and falling gulls.

Mexico vanishes in the smoke dissipating
in the twilight sky.

Visions of Manhattan dance,
like miniature whirlwinds,
in the hearts of the Mexicanos.

In the lightless, clandestine depths of steerage,
Rafael opens a wooden box.
It contains a picture of his parents,
a pencil sketch of Presidente Álvaro Obregón,
and a small flag of Mexico.

Rafael picks up and kisses each item,
then carefully puts them back.

On the third midnight of the voyage,
on el Día de los Muertos,
Rafael tosses the cherished box into the sea.

---

steerage: immigrants who came to the United States from overseas during the late nineteenth and early twentieth centuries often traveled in the cheap steerage sections of steamships, so named because the compartments were located near the steering mechanism of the ships. **Presidente Álvaro Obregón:** (1880-1928) president of Mexico, 1920-1924. **Día de los Muertos:** Day of the Dead, celebrated every November 2, commemorates the souls of departed loved ones.

What are the Fortunes telling us?

Ciudad de Nueva York.
La Primavera, 1924.

The Mexican *tabaqueros*—
father, mother, and three darling boys—
spend six days and half of Sunday
each week
squinting in dim yellow light,
rolling and wrapping cigars,
and stuffing them, like dumb fishes,
into little tin cans.

The Mexican immigrants, five months out of Vera Cruz,
spend entire days
in the oppressive stink of tobacco,
an awful smell that eats into the soul.

Each night, near midnight, in the harsh glare
of a single naked electric light bulb,
Mamita reads penny fortune cards.

In halting and broken English she reads the cards out loud.

She has no idea what the Fortunes
are telling her.

Ciudad de Nueva York: New York City. **Primavera, 1924:** Spring, 1924. *tabaqueros:* tobacco workers who stuff, label, and package cigars. **Vera Cruz:** Mexican port city.

The peddler of artificial flowers

Manhattan, 1925.

Mamita leaves the tenement every day at dawn.
She posts bills on telephone poles and lampposts
throughout a radius of ten blocks.

Her fliers advertise her gorgeous flowers,
blooming in all the colors of the rainbow;
flowers that need no attention, no water,
and never die.

Mamita advertises her wire-stemmed, paper-petal flowers
in Spanish that the Italians, Jews, and Greeks cannot read.

But each day customers mill about her makeshift stand.
And every day the entire harvest is sold.

Los lavaplatos

These men, without names, without papers,
scour the flatware,
for hours, for days without end,
in the humid steam of the kitchens.

They come and go seven days each week.
They are invisible. They have no histories.
No one knows what they dream.

Every day there are whole harvests of forks and spoons
to pick and clean.
Dishes swim in seas of soapy water.

The dishwashers, themselves, swirl in soap and water.
Their lives swirl down into the drains.

Los lavaplatos: The dishwashers. **These men, without names, without papers:** Immigrants who entered the United States without papers (or documents).

Los Yunaites Estaites

Zeferino, fresh from Sonora,
marvels at the electric Red Cars and automobiles
as they nose forward under sun and moon.

He stands breathless before the rising metropolis.
He is lost and giddy beneath the dreamlike skyline.

Zeferino sees Southern California
as the sunkissed Promised Land.
He gives his heart to Los Yunaites Estaites,
rejoicing in la colonia con los recién llegados,
un México de afuera.

But he still weeps for la madre patria.

El ciudad es un caleidoscopio de fantasías:
Mexican boleros from KELW shower Chávez Ravine
and Brooklyn Heights.

Workers smile and cry as Los Hermanos Bañuelos sing, sultrily, "El Lavaplatos."

Nuestra Señora rises above the churches and tire factories.
She takes the hands of seamstresses and tortilla makers
and leads them closer to paradise.

Images of Lupe Velez and Dolores del Rio flicker on the silver screen.
En las cantinas men speak softly
of the bittersweet mysteries of love.

The First Street Bridge sways in the sundown heat.

There's a full house at El Teatro Zendéjas,

lovers dance in La Placita,
and nobody is lonely in the barrios tonight.

Zeferino loves his home in the city of Angelinos,
but aches for a living wage
as he watches the silver moon swim through a sea of stars.

Sonora: state in northern México. **electric Red Cars:** electric trolley cars. **Los Yunaites Estaites:** informal Mexicano name for Los Estados Unidos, the United States. **la colonia con los recién llegados, un México de afuera:** the colony (neighborhood) with the recent arrivals (from México), a México outside México. **la madre patria:** the motherland. **El ciudad es un caleidoscopio de fantasías:** The city is a kaleidoscope of fantasies. **KELW:** radio station in Burbank that broadcast Spanish-language news and music in the 1920s. **Chávez Ravine and Brooklyn Heights:** Mexican neighborhoods in Los Angeles. **"El Lavaplatos":** "The Dishwasher," a song about the obstacles faced by Mexican-American workers by **Los Hermanos Bañuelos:** Mexican-American musical group. **Nuestra Señora:** Our Lady, The Blessed Virgin Mary. **Lupe Velez:** (1908-1944) Mexican-American film star. **Dolores del Rio:** (1908-1983) Mexican-American motion picture star. **las cantinas:** bars. **The First Street Bridge:** in East Los Angeles. **El Teatro Zendéjas:** theater on South Spring Street in Los Angeles, which presented plays and other artistic performances to predominately Mexican audiences. **La Placita:** in Downtown Los Angeles. **barrios:** Mexican neighborhoods. **Angelinos:** residents of Los Angeles.

The Flats

The sun rises over the Flats,
this little kingdom of homes
made from hammered-out cans,
old boxes, and burlap.

Here a few tired Tin Lizzies honk hoarsely
at dogs and goats that scavenge gloriously in stark dirt roads.

La Virgencita, the blessed queen of the Flats,
appears in the morning sunburst.
She is resplendent.
She is clothed in the actual rays of the sun.

Nuestra Señora la Reina de los Ángeles,
la Madre de Dios,
blesses her children, their animals,
their beautiful cactus gardens.

Every living thing in the Flats is made blessed
by her eternal mercy.

Maybe in unguarded moments,
even the unbelievers among us drop their hearts
into this sea of sunlight.

---

the Flats: a Mexican-American barrio just east of the Los Angeles River. **Tin Lizzies:** Ford Model-T automobiles. **la Virgencita:** the Blessed Virgin Mary. **Nuestra Señora la Reina de los Ángeles, / la Madre de Dios:** Our Lady the Queen of the Angels, / the Mother of God: the Blessed Virgin Mary.

A luminous glow

The sun settles peacefully into the Los Angeles River,
leaving a luminous glow, a sacred light, in the sky.

What does this light indicate to them
who see their next home in the heavens?

In the twilight, the electric lights come on;
they blink boldly along Boyle Avenue.

Who knows how many people have come,
and gone, along these streets?

Could it be that their ghosts are with us now
in Boyle Heights, Belvedere, and Hollenbeck?

On Figueroa Street, the automobiles
and trolley cars stop. The clocks stop.
The world stops spinning.
No words dance on anyone's lips.
Even the animals are silent.
There are no noises anywhere.
This is a silence as old as the world.

Who can say there are no ghosts among us?

Who really believes that our ancestors have left us here alone?

Boyle Avenue: in the Boyle Heights section of Los Angeles. **Boyle Heights, Belvedere, and Hollenbeck:** neighborhoods (or barrios) that became East Angeles. **Figueroa Street:** in Downtown Los Angeles.

Aquí se habla español

Zeferino smiles in Sonoratown
every time a missionary approaches him
about this faith or that faith.

The gabachos prowl these streets,
searching for converts.

They live to missionize and proselytize.

They yearn to shepherd the flock away from the Holy Faith,
that crossroads where Mexica deities meet the Mother of God.

They come here with English strangely dancing,
almost writhing,
on their lips.

How they ache to raise the Mexicans up
from their lethargy,
and prod them out of their inertness.

A twinkle flourishes in Zeferino's eye
each time an apostle tells him
he'll find health and wealth as soon as he takes a drink
from the great mainstream.

Aquí se habla español: Here we speak Spanish. **Sonoratown:** name for the Mexicano barrio, centered on the old plaza, in the downtown district of Los Angeles, slightly west of the Los Angeles River. Many Mexican immigrants from the state of Sonora were residents of the area. **every time a missionary approaches:** in the 1910s and 1920s, an "Americanization" campaign was conducted in Los Angeles barrios by civic organizations and Protestant missionaries. The Americanizers sought to teach English and instill "American values" in the Mexican residents while missionaries tried to convert Mexicans to various Protestant denominations. The Americanization movement largely failed as most Mexicans were determined to maintain their Spanish language, Catholic faith, and

Mexican customs and mores. **gabachos:** gringos; Anglos. **the flock:** Mexican-American Catholics living in Los Angeles barrios. **the Holy Faith / that crossroads where Mexica deities meet the Mother of God:** the Holy Faith refers to the Roman Catholic faith; in this case, Mexican Catholicism which blends native religious beliefs and practices with European Catholicism.

Account of the Miraculous Apparition
of the Holy Image of the Virgin of Guadalupe
in Boyle Heights, California

December 12, 1934.

Mexicanos burn a crucifix into a frozen sun.

These lambs and lions heave tumultuously up Boyle Avenue
like waves of heat, or untrammeled radio waves.

These sanctified immigrants sing and dance
on the outskirts of Heaven.

They prance with their ancestral ghosts
and frolic with the saints.

The magic and mystifications of Mexico sparkle and scintillate
in the traffic and clamor east of Los Angeles,
and the street lamps and telephone poles are silent sentinels
keeping watch
over the boiling, bubbling melting pot.

The Mexicans chant their blessings to the Holy Father
while passers-by snarl and sneer and long for quieter days.

But these penitents sing, like thunder, in the streets
as Mexico is reborn
under the Los Angeles skyline.

A sundial indicates High Noon,

but the hour is irrelevant.
No time matters: *¡Estamos en las manos de Dios!*

If this were Judgment Day,
the feast in Boyle Heights would go on, unabated.

Account of the Miraculous Apparition of the Holy Image of the Virgin of Guadalupe in Boyle Heights, California: This title is modeled after Fray Mateo de la Cruz' *Account of the Miraculous Apparition of the Holy Image of the Virgin of Guadalupe of Mexico,* published in 1660. **December 12, 1934:** On December 12, 1934, Mexican-American Catholics organized a massive religious procession along Boyle Avenue in the East L.A. barrio of Boyle Heights. The procession commemorated El Día de la Virgen de Guadalupe. As many as 40,000 participants turned out in the largest demonstration of any kind in the history of Los Angeles up until that time. The grand parade included a beautiful reenactment of the Virgin's appearance before Juan Diego in 1531. Please see the poem "Nuestra Señora de Guadalupe and visions of the new kingdom in Mexico." **melting pot:** the dubious metaphor that diverse ethnicities merge into a single American character. **Holy Father:** the pope. Pope Pius XI (r.1922-1939) was the reigning Roman Catholic pontiff in 1934. **passers-by sneer and snarl and long for quieter days:** The unrestricted, public celebration of Mexican Catholicism in the streets of Los Angles barrios was absolutely exhilarating for those Mexican immigrants who had suffered during anti-religious persecutions in Mexico in the 1920s. However, some Anglo observers commented that the 1934 Mexican-American Catholic procession was dangerous religious fanaticism unleashed on the streets of Los Angeles. *¡Estamos en las manos de Dios!:* The December 12, 1934 demonstration included emotional chants of "¡Viva Cristo Rey!"—"Long Live Christ the King!" Some celebrants carried aloft signs which read: "Estamos en las manos de Dios": "We are in the hands of God."

Our hearts are pulled elsewhere

We have to be Americans. We shall be. We shall learn English. We shall love America, and help to build America. We shall accomplish in the New World a hundred times more than we could in the old. But you shall not be able to erase the old home from your heart. Your heart will be drawn elsewhere. And in your solitude, images will rise up and stare in your faces with eternal sorrow.
★ABRAHAM CAHAN

In La Loma, Bishop, Palo Verde,
the colonies of our adopted land,
we open shops and tend gardens.

We hear holy birds singing in las iglesias católicas.

We have splashed rainbow images of the Virgin all over the horizon.

We harvest beautiful flowers
and build the San Bernardino Freeway through the heart
of Los Angeles.

We sing in Spanish and English.

We love America and raise the sun over America.

But our hearts are pulled elsewhere.

La Loma, Bishop, Palo Verde: three neighborhoods in Chávez Ravine in Los Angeles, now the site of Dodger Stadium. **las iglesias católicas:** the Catholic churches.

Los deportados

Hoy traen la gran polvareda / y sin consideración / mujeres, niños, y ancianos / nos llevan a la frontera, / nos echan de esta nación.

All over Los Angeles, signs snort: NO MEN WANTED.

Bread lines and soup lines
      wrap around
the city's blocks,
and the Salvation Army has hordes to feed.

"Nobody knows you when you're down and out."

"Brother, can you spare a dime?"

Here is a cruel, cruel moon that throws her light
over the City of Angels.

Everyone is bathed in moonlight.
Where can we hide now? Where is a darkened corner?

The Border Patrol and the Police give thanks for this luminous moon
that traps these aliens,
this riff-raff,
these undesirables.

La Opinión and the archbishop plea for justice,
but Mexicanos are herded into boxcars and shipped out into the twilight.

Tears water the railroad lines from Los Angeles County
to the Mexican border.

Hoy traen la gran polvareda: A popular 1930s *corrido,* or, folk ballad. In English: "Today they bring great disturbance / and without consideration / women, children, and old ones / they take us to the border, / they eject us from this nation." **Los deportados:** Mexican deportees, repatriated during the Depression era. **"Nobody knows you when you're down and out" "Brother, can you spare a dime?":** Popular and somber

Depression-era songs. ***La Opinión:*** Los Angeles Spanish-language newspaper. **the archbishop:** Roman Catholic Archbishop John J. Cantwell of Los Angeles. Cantwell served as bishop and archbishop of the Los Angeles diocese and archdiocese from 1917 to 1947. **They are herded into boxcars:** Mexican *deportados* were deported to Mexico aboard Southern Pacific Railroad boxcars.

La luna azul

Tonight the whole world is blue.
Blue. Blue. Blue.
In the light of the blue moon,
      we dance through Lincoln Heights.

The telephone lines hum inaudible songs
and God, himself, sighs in our ears.

The world is spinning aimlessly
through the Kingdom of Heaven.

I hear East L.A. singing

Summer 1941

The birds in the murals chirp to each epiphany
that rises,
like helium balloons,
over the earth.

Women and children sing in the churches
to a brown-skinned Christ,
who hands them luminous birds.

There are no chrysanthemums in East Los Angeles,
but cans, car tires, and corrugated tin are flowers that bloom rainbows
in the morning mist.

By noon, the city is bathed in life.

Boys lick cherry ices.
They do battle on diamonds of dirt and grass.

Priests and nuns wrap tamales,
and cook menudo and pozole on old stoves.

The late afternoon is a sea of dreamy blue.

Neighbors gather in the evening and talk till the small hours of the morning.
They sigh about life in México under Manuel Avila Camacho.
They long for Cárdenas.

Mothers and fathers hum their chicitas into the kingdom of dreams.

Mariachi music leaps and dances from little houses.
Corridos traipse down back alleys,

boleros ache in a blue moon.

La gente, nuestra familia.

La Virgen de Guadalupe stands with cactus and eagle in East L.A.

A slight scent of cinnamon,
and the Earth tilts toward heaven.

I hear East L.A. singing: The title of this poem is inspired by Walt Whitman's poem "I hear America singing." **diamonds of dirt and grass:** baseball diamonds. **tamale:** minced and seasoned meat packed in cornmeal dough and wrapped in cornhusks and steamed. **menudo:** beef tripe soup. **pozole:** native hominy. **Manuel Avila Camacho:** (1897-1955) Mexican president, 1940-1946. **Cárdenas: Lázaro Cárdenas:** (1895-1970) Mexican president, 1934-1940. His social reforms made him extremely popular among poorer Mexicanos. **chicitas:** little girls. **corridos:** Mexican folk ballads. **La gente, nuestra familia:** The people, our family. **La Virgen de Guadalupe:** The Virgin of Guadalupe, the Blessed Virgin Mary. **cactus and eagle:** symbols of the Mexican nation.

Boyle Heights, East Los Angeles, Lincoln Heights

New Years' Eve 1942

The planets, in their lonesome orbits,
ring in the new year.

The planets are infinitely lonely in their cold exile.

But the stars—beautiful hot embers—
shimmer and shingaling
in the blue light of midnight.

Tonight, there is no loneliness in the City of Angels.

La gente wave Mexican flags and U.S. flags and cheer,
dancing on the shores of a new year.

The people bathe in a river of song:
Elenita Salinas is singing on the radio,
and two lovers are about to cry.

Mariachi bands serenade las mujeres,
who recover los corazones perdidos.

Handsome bronze pachucos drink ice cold Coca-Colas and smolder in heat
as they seduce beautiful angels.

Birds-of-paradise stick their gorgeous, dumb heads
toward the majestic moon.

Tonight the stars dance gloriously beyond our grasp.

---

shingaling: to dance and sing. **City of Angels:** Los Angeles. **La gente:** The people.
Elenita Salinas: Mexican-American recording artist popular during the 1940s. **las mujeres:** the women. **los corazones perdidos:** the lost hearts. **pachucos:** young
Mexican-American males, sometimes members of gangs and believed to be "punks" by
some observers.

The tealeaves tell us nothing

Anthony counts the ominous clouds
and braids them into his sister's hair.

He conjures up poems from hot Santa Ana winds
and feverish dreams.

He paints poems in dusky watercolors.

Today, the dead stay away. They don't come near us.
They have their own reasons, and they're not saying a word.

The world seems to sigh in the heavy sunset.

Tonight, fortunetellers divine nothing from tealeaves.
They're in the dark, like everyone else.

There can be no prognostication.
It's all in the hands of God.

The Sleepy Lagoon incident

East Los Angeles, August 1, 1942.

Los pachucos gather at the reservoir
to drink and talk.

They sing in their anonymity.

These pachucos, with their shirts off, are cocky.
They breathe fire in the City of Angels.
They grunt like bulls.
    These boys are gladiators.
They are lovers, poets, altar boys, and grandsons.

Some wish for peace;
    some want to take the world apart at the seams.

In a feverish hour, they wrestle and punch and slash.

These boys are drenched in their manhood.

Sleepy Lagoon: On August 1, 1942, Mexican-American gangs clashed at Sleepy Lagoon, a reservoir located in East Los Angeles. One Mexican-American boy died in the
fighting. The Los Angeles Police Department arrested the entire 38th Street Club. The
trial was patently unjust and became the source of Mexican-American and liberal
agitation.

In the mood

From the Flats and Boyle Heights,
        from the heart of East L.A.,
pachucos strut in felt hats,
draped coats,
and baggy pants.

Some sport ducktail haircuts.

These zoot suiters are real cool cats.

With their pachuquitas on their arms,
they swirl and swing to Glenn Miller.

They ache gleefully from Mexican boleros.

These beautiful boys from the barrios
have trumpets lamenting, saxophones sobbing
in their heads.

The man in the moon sighs for a zoot suit
and one lovely night of jitterbugging.

From the battle carriers and cruisers,
        from the docks of San Pedro and Long Beach,
sailors, smart and spiffy in their sailor boy suits,
flood into L.A. in search of a good time.

On furlough, these sailors seek fantasy in the City of Angels:
they saunter down Sunset and Vine,
        along a trail of moonlight,
hoping for a dreamy night with a silver screen starlet!

On the streets of Hollywood,

they hope for a brush against Mr. Gable,
a few idle words with Bogey,
or a chance encounter with the Brown Bomber.

These are good men,
who've put their lives on the line for their country,
who face horrors on the sea
unimaginable.

On leave, they'll blow off steam.

They ache for a good time.

Boys need to be boys.

The Flats, Boyle Heights, East L.A.: Mexican-American neighborhoods in Los Angeles. **pachucos:** young Mexican-American males. **felt hats, draped coats and baggy pants. . .ducktail haircuts:** During the early 1940s, young Mexican-American males imitated the look of mobsters and African-American jitterbuggers, establishing a distinctive look for young males from Los Angeles barrios. **pachuquitas:** little pachucas; the girlfriends of the pachucos. **Glenn Miller:** (1904-1944) U.S. trombone player, big band leader. One of his classic swing songs is the title of this poem. **jitterbugging:** popular dance of the early 1940s, performed primarily to boogie-woogie and swing music. **sailors. . .flood into L.A. in search of a good time:** In June 1943, U.S. servicemen, mainly sailors, arrived in Los Angeles on brief furloughs. Pachucos clashed with sailors over young Mexican-American women. Large numbers of sailors retaliated by attacking Mexican-American zoot-suiters in their own barrios. **Mr. Gable:** Clark Gable (1901-1960) U.S. film actor. **Bogey:** Humphrey Bogart (1899-1957) U.S. film actor. **Brown Bomber:** Joe Louis (1914-1981) U.S. boxer, heavyweight champion, 1937-1949.

Boy wars

Streetcars swim in the humid air.

Apparitions swarm through the Hollywood Hills.

The City of Angels seems under the influence of a planet
that will not let it sleep.

Pachucos and sailors lock horns over pachuquitas
and the tinderbox blows to kingdom come.

A frenzy of fists, flash of knives,
and war spills out into the streets.
The prowess of boys mirrors fire unleashed.
Spray of sweat, dance of blood,
and the sky itself seems bruised and lacerated.

Tire irons speak their own Scripture.

Sailors storm the barrios.
They drag vatos from streetcars and movie theaters.

Pachucos are beaten,
        pummeled like piñatas.

G.I.s chop ducktails. They spit in faces,
and tear off the pants of pachucos,
exposing bronze moons, magnificent moons.

An orgy of greaser stomping.

Fantasies of domination played out
in darkened alleyways.

Boy wars: The Los Angeles press called clashes between young U.S. sailors and young Mexican-American zoot-suiters in Los Angeles in June 1943 "boy wars." **The City of Angels seems under the influence of a planet:** This line is a paraphrase of a 1537 statement about Honduras by Francisco De Montejo, the Spanish governor of Honduras: "I don't know what will happen to this land, but it seems under the influence of a planet that will not let it sleep." **pachuquitas:** little pachucas; girlfriends of the pachucos. **vatos:** guys; dudes. **An orgy of greaser stomping:** Anglos called the raids by sailors on zoot-suiters in Los Angeles barrios "greaser stomping." Some historians have suggested a homoerotic element to the G.I. attacks on young Mexican-American men.

Love is just a glance away

[A contemplation after a dream night with the 38th Street Club,
a tribe of young Mexican-American males in the early 1940s.]

These boys talk so casually about falling in love,
they make it seem as if it's a daily occurrence.
Why, I never heard of something so outlandish!
I am supposed to believe that these boys find lovers
lurking around every street corner,
that love is just a glance away?

These boys tell me that they are poets
who paint their songs, like vibrant murals,
on the walls of churches and police stations.
Well let me tell you this: I was not born yesterday;
no, you cannot sell me the First Street Bridge.
I will not buy that bill of goods.
Imagine that! The search for love and solace so easy
that these boys don't even break a sweat.

First Street Bridge: in East Los Angeles, California.

El día después de mañana

Me voy a levantár
y danzaré,
solo levantarme como un fénix bailando una danza de resurección. . .

Con todos mirandome,
voy a danzár como un fénix brillante,

     quemando un hoyo por la noche.

_____

The English translation follows: "I'm gonna get up / and dance, / just rise like a phoenix dancing a resurrection dance. . . // With everyone watching, / I'm gonna dance like a bright phoenix, // burning a hole through the night."

A democracy of ghosts

México, with thorns

A sugar sun is all we have left
from this heaven on earth.

Dust claims everything else:
Dusky moon and winter solstice in the kingdom of dust.

Utopia is a blown husk.
A receding mist. Paradise is no man's land.

This is our world of bones
and banana dreams.

Our empire of tears, rain,
bundles of hurricanes,
sugar cane;
     our kingdom
of papier-mâché flowers, a paper sun,
toy burros,
     toy Christ;
our México, our bowl of sorrow.

We have the eclipse,
the dusky icons,
muddied myths,
the ambush,
la guerra,
the burial.

Nuestro país that makes a sunset
of our hearts.

---

la guerra: the war. **Nuestro país:** Our country.

A cascade of light

Madero, you apostle of liberty!
You emerged from cascading light
and handed us democracy, like a chrysanthemum.

The Porfiriato crumbled
in the white heat of desire.

Francisco, are you still writing poems
in heaven?

Francisco Madero: (1873-1913) Mexican president, 1911-1913. **Porfiriato:** the age of Porfirio, the thirty-five year dictatorship of Mexican President Porfirio Díaz. In 1910, revolutionary and author and idealist Francisco I. Madero proclaimed the Díaz regime illegitimate and, the following year, engineered a revolution which toppled the dictator from power. Madero was proclaimed provisional president. He was assassinated on February 22, 1913, on the order of Mexican General Victoriano Huerta (1854-1916), who became president of Mexico, 1913-1914.

The haciendas divided

The revolution has not triumphed. In your hands is the will and the power to save it; but if, unfortunately, you do not, the shades of Cuauhtémoc, Hidalgo, and Juárez and the heroes of all time will stir in their graves to ask: What have you done with the blood of your brothers?

★ Emiliano Zapata

Emiliano Zapata dreams a red flag snapping
in the wind over Cuernevaca.

Zapata can almost see the haciendas divided
and the mines and railroads in the hands of the poor.

Emiliano can just about see sunlight blossoming
across the face of México.

He dreams Quetzalcóatl rising
from a stack of bones.

He swears he sees the falling eagle,
the setting sun;

Zapata sees the lifeline end in his hand.

Emiliano Zapata: (1877?-1919) Mexican revolutionary, agrarian reformer, and guerrilla leader, whose battle cry was "Land, liberty, and death to the landholders." Zapata was assassinated in Chinameca, Ayala on April 10, 1919. **Quetzalcóatl:** Mexica deity who promised a new reign of peace on earth.

Ten years washed away

The forest is yours. Go on and make charcoal. . .get to work. Enough is enough!
Forget the Revolution. What's done is done! Whoever is dead, is dead! Those
that are left, are left! So, go on, get to work. Make charcoal and go and sell it.
> ★ Colonel Jesús Montoya

Beat your swords into plowshares and till your fields.
Grow your wheat or soy beans.
If you raise sugar cane,
cut and sell it.
Feed your chickens.
The Revolution is over!

Madero, Zapata, Carranza, Villa are dead.
A million have died,
their ghosts are stuffed inside the hollow moon.

Martyrs have nothing to tell us;
they whisper nothing from the other side.
Leave the dead to the dead.
So, go on, take care of your children.
Ground your flour.
Sing your hosannas and dance beneath the soft, blue light of the stars.

Forget the Revolution;
what has been done will never be undone.

Ten years washed away: The Mexican Revolution was waged from 1910 to 1920.
Madero, Zapata, Carranza, Villa: Francisco I. Madero (1873-1913) Mexican revolutionist and president, (1911-1913); Emiliano Zapata (1877?-1919) Mexican revolutionary; Venustiano Carranza (1859-1920) Mexican revolutionist and president, (1915-1920); Francisco (Pancho) Villa (1878-1923) Mexican revolutionary leader. Madero, Zapata, Carranza, and Villa were killed by assassination.

Cardenistas and visions of the new republic in México, 1934-1940

There is one thing that our oppressors should understand well: today, the Mexican people are willing to die in order to defend their rights; and it is not that they want to incinerate the national territory with a revolution, it is that they are no longer afraid of the sacrifice.

★FRANCISCO I. MADERO, *PLAN DE SAN LUIS POTOSÍ* [1910]

México is a shadow nation

A country of cold wind

A totalitarianism of ghosts.

But Ignatio Espitia, in
Zamora,
     sees Christ risen
in Cárdenas,
Lázaro come back from the dead.

In Chinameca,
Policarpo swears he saw Zapata's ghost in the sunrise.
He said Emiliano's spirit turned from smoke
to radiant light.

Across the motherland, peasants rejoice
in liberation.
Animals and flowers are more beautiful.
The rocks, themselves, begin to sing.

Shadows lift from roots and towering totems.
Ghosts thrive in the light of the shattered stars.

Roses once again thrive in winter
and the Image of the Blessed Mother appears on Lázarus's tilma.

At Cuatrociénegas,

los comunistas smash gold icons
against the mountain,
burn crates of money,
and incinerate the root of all evil.

Zapatistas, at Soconusco,
        machine-gun los adversarios,
los capitalistas,
                los enemigos:
blood splattered on the moon.

The colors of a holocaust always fade in a brilliant sun.

And sorrow cracks like a dried cornhusk.

Peace over moon   pyramid   ejido.

Peace grips México D.F.   And peace kisses Chichimeca.
Cárdenas nurtures the state at the roots of justice.
Light plucked from thorns.
La primavera.
Ghosts dance around the altar.

And México has entered into a house of Heaven.

Ignatio Espitia: Cárdenista campesino born on a Zamora-area hacienda. **Chinameca:** site of Emiliano Zapata's assassination in 1919. **Cárdenas:** Lázaro Cárdenas del Río (1895-1970) Mexican general and political leader; president of México, 1934-1940. President Cárdenas was one of the most forceful of the Latin American nationalists, expropriating foreign petroleum interests and redistributing 40 million acres of land to Mexican peasants. **los comunistas:** the (Mexican) communists. The Mexican Communist party (PCM-Partido Comunista Mexicana) was founded in 1919 and formally dissolved in 1981. **los adversarios:** the adversaries. **los capitalistas:** the capitalists. **los enemigos:** the enemies. **ejido:** common lands occupied by peasants. **La primavera:** The spring.

Las nubes mexicanes

The mango trees bend, slightly, in the sunset:
There is peace from Tampico
to Acapulco. A quiet, immaculate calm has taken the kingdom.
Sé que esta paz es eterna.

Stone idols swirl in a wash of stars.

Women paint poems: visions of God and azure *splashed*
on whole parts of the earth.

A green flash after sunset;
swirl of dusk wind, sweep of silence,
and the world drifts in the cool green light. . .

Tonight we can remake México,
rebirthing her from fire and glacial ice,
a resurrection from trampled flowers and melted moons.

We can remake our country
from the hearts of our ancestors.

A half moon burns over the quiet sea.

    A phantom world falls from the clouds
and turns
      in our eyes.

Turquoise fire smoldering in our souls.

At last we can face each other
in peace,

with our hearts rushing toward the moonlight.

Armies retreat at our music blowing softly
against the twilight.

And no love falters. . .

<hr/>

Las nubes mexicanes: the Mexican clouds. **Sé que esta paz es eterna:** I know this peace is eternal.

A dance of shadows

The old moon faces Guadalajara.

Mexica ruins weather another century.

No incense burns near the pillaged rice, shattered obsidian,
but the dead cities flower in eternal light.

Cárdenas left the little suns and moons shining
in the sacred places.

His decrees gave land to the poor;
he decreed liberty to the unions.

Los socialistas sang in the moon.

Los indigenistas painted Cárdenas's image in volcanic ash,
the residue of primordial fire.

After Cárdenas, the burning of poems,
the death of birds.

A dance of shadows.

México, a folded flower.

Cárdenas: Lázaro Cárdenas del Río (1895-1970) president of México, 1934-1940. **Los socialistas:** The socialists. **Los indigenistas:** The indigenous peoples.

The deepest part of the sea

The promise of the Revolution is lost somewhere
between dark clouds
and the sea.

Avila Camacho spins rainbows,
paints sunrises,
    but there are no doctors in Pijijapin.
In Nogales, Nueva Casas Grandes, Ciudad Insurgentes,
there have been no new wells dug for drinking water,
no land distributed,
    y pues nada.

There's only empty starlight at Ahualulco.

The sugar of Morelos,
      the chickpeas of Sonora,
        Coahuila's cotton
do not reconcile the peasants with the sunrise.

The poor, twice as beautiful as the sun,
ache for the mouth of the cornucopia
and peace in the moonrise.

The peasants pray for México, una sunrisa,
una basílica,
uno sacramento.

But their hopes are dropped
into the deepest part of the sea.

Avila Camacho: Manuel Avila Camacho (1897-1955), Mexican president, 1940-1946. **Pi-jijapin. . .Nogales, Nueva Casas Grandes, Ciudad Insurgentes:** in México. **y pues nada:** and nothing. **Ahualulco. . .Morelos. . .Sonora. . .Coahuila:** in México.

A lost benevolence; a benevolence never known

In Acapulco, Presidente Miguel Alemán
bathes in a darling sun.
He has a spectacular moon over Mazatlán.

Alemán has never understood
what's coming down for México;
     he's never figured out that the frayed tether snaps
under the weight of poverty and despair.

"The peasants can ache just a little bit longer."

And rice is not meat.
Neither rice nor maize is meat.
Y la tierra de los monopolistas es no nuestra tierra.

We do not know how to rub the pain from our hearts.

Miguel Alemán: (1902-1983) Mexican president, 1946-1952. **Y la tierra de los monopolistas es no nuestra tierra:** And the land of the monopolists is not our land.

A democracy of ghosts

Before the covenant rusted
    to metal scrap,
the United States was gilded with the dawn,
glutted with sunrise:
        but all the promise now become
    a spent sun:

In the Coachella and Imperial Valleys,
       the children eat dirt at the end of the rainbow.

Only with certain colors
can you paint a democracy consuming itself,
like a snake gripping its tail in its mouth.

Consuelo holds María in her arms
as the sun rakes Calexico. Consuelo keeps a poem
under her breath
even though the dust turns Calexico to hell.

A long road. A skyway of dusty Sundays.
Caked mud.
15 dollars.
No home.
So the United States leaves promise burning
like gasoline barrels in the heart.

Our Lady of Guadalupe kisses the poor,
who cup in their hands only the dark dancing of clouds.

The faces of the poor swim through paradise.
Wilted hearts dropped along the border.

A hard road. Canaan in sight?
    Mexicanos see it in California.
    Some swear they've touched it;

some are trigger-happy to touch it;
most lose heart,
       a world slipping
through their fingers.

From Brawley:
     south to El Centro, to East Mesa,
          souls are smeared along the horizon like sunsets;
          a democracy of ghosts;
          an eternity eaten by wolves.

The cruelty of rainbows

Braceros call México *Sal si puedes:*
        Get out while you can.

Braceros see storm clouds brood over México,
they see a rainbow bloom over the U.S.

Rainbows are cruel things:
so much beauty, exquisite colors you can never touch.

December 31, 1949.
100 Mexicanos "illegally" enter the rainbow.
They seek the prize.
A feel of the Promised Land.
To live and love under spacious skies.

But the hearts of the poor
swim in the lettuce and spinach fields of Salinas.
Magic and poverty rise like mushroom clouds
over the San Joaquín Valley,
where children dance through purgatory under a lavender moon.

In San Pedro, Antonia gets pennies
canning fruits and vegetables
        for Del Monte.
    She holds a hollow sun in her hands.
Her heart holds holy fire.

In East L.A., Mamá besa a sus queridos.
Mamá lays the sun upon their heads.
        She tells them not to cry.
Mamá tiene la santísima trinidad;
    she has her santa cruces, but can't find
Nuestra Señora on 3rd Street.

So the question becomes:

Is promise EVER fulfilled in the heart?
Diego doesn't really know
        and yo no lo sé, pero las mujeres les cuentan a sus niños
that life is better
                en los Estados Unidos. . .

And Consuelo doesn't argue.
She had too much dirt in Tabasco.
Too much broken pottery.
So now, she thinks, she's got the dawn
wrapped up in Santa María, California.

Let her think that.
Illusions, like rainbows, can warm the heart.

Braceros: Mexican-born railroad and agricultural workers employed in the United States from World War II to 1964. **Mamá besa a sus queridos:** Mama kisses her little darlings. **la santísima trinidad:** the Holy Trinity. **santa cruces:** sacred crosses. **Nuestra Señora:** Our Lady, the Blessed Virgin Mary. **yo no sé, pero las mujeres les cuentan a sus niños:** I don't know, but the women tell their children. **los Estados Unidos:** the United States. **Tabasco:** a state in México.

When October becomes rain
(Nunca la muerte)

Families from Ensenada,
Zacatecas, Matamoros,
        Tijuana,
Ciudad Obregón,
    "wetbacks" to the americanos
and los gringos call 'em "greasers"
who live by elbow grease and back break
    and dreams always underfoot,
never in hand, in the tomato rows.

Sorrow like a sunset.

Acre on acre of cabbage, broccoli,
sugar beets. An empire of peaches and grapes.

Dreams are palsied in the search for profit;
hearts are parched in the fields and gutted in the canneries.

The faces of migrants are not reflected
in iceberg lettuce; souls are not preserved
by olive-root nor lemon-root.

Farm workers are not sheltered when October becomes rain;
a month of storm;
a deluge.

California has become ten days of unremitting rains,

flooding our hearts.

Bracero bones burn in the cold.
Generation and generation
under blue paler than heartache.

La raza, nuestra raza, caught in the years of freezing fire,
years of rising poison, pero no muere,
nunca la muerte, *nunca la muerte*.

---

wetbacks: undocumented Mexican immigrants. **greasers:** derogatory name for Mexicanos. **La raza, nuestra raza:** The race, our race. **no muerte, / nunca la muerte:** no death, / never death.

Emma Tenayuca walks away from the crowd

The masses marvel at seas of money,
sprawling homes,
and automobiles that glide like aluminum fish.

The splendid possessions are worshiped
on bended knee and lustful heart.

On the scales,
nothing is weightier than gold.

The crowd venerates star and titan
while the faces of farm workers drain to bleached moonlight.

Emma Tenayuca walks away with empty hands
and her heart brought blessed to the Lord.

Emma Tenayuca: (1916-1999) Mexican-American labor activist and U.S. Communist leader. Tenyauca organized a strike of pecan workers in San Antonio, Texas in 1937. She was blacklisted as a consequence of her work in the Communist Party (which was established in 1919). She moved to San Francisco, where she earned her teacher's certificate. Tenayuca eventually returned to San Antonio to teach, retiring in 1982. Emma Tenayuca died on July 23, 1999. **star and titan:** Hollywood film stars and business moguls.

La Migra

Take steps at this very hour that our frontiers be fenced in by barriers. . .that not a single soul pass o'er the border, that not a hare be able to run or a crow to fly.
    ★ALEKSANDR PUSHKIN

La Migra leaves no stone unturned;
every cactus shadow is searched,
and checked again.

The U.S. Border Patrol stops and frisks the wildcats and roadrunners.

God willing, no wetback will cross this border.

La Migra demands even the jack rabbits
to show I.D.

La Migra: United States Border Patrol (established in 1924). **Aleksandr Pushkin:** quote from Pushkin's work *Boris Godenuv* (published, 1837).

Las enganchistas

The agricultural fields of California stretch out
to the ends of the earth.

Here the land has no beginning
and no end.

The sun and winds conspire
to turn the earth into hell.

Las enganchistas salivate like Pavlov's dogs
at every prospect of coin.

Dollar signs dance in their heads like sugarplums.

Las enganchistas: Labor recruiters hired by U.S. agricultural, mining, and railroad firms to bring Mexican immigrants into the U.S. Southwest. The *enganchistas* (also known as *contratistas*) took a sizable portion of the wages of the Mexican immigrant workers who they had brought into the United States. In some instances, *enganchistas* absconded with all of their workers' wages.

Los indocumentados

When an alien resides with you in your land, you shall not do him wrong. You shall treat the alien who resides with you no differently than the natives born among you; have the same love for him as for yourself.
    ★ LEVITICUS 19:33-34

Operation Wetback, 1954.

The angels with broken hearts
lay their burdens down at the stone wall.

The moon with a bruised face lets her sorrow free.

In the San Gabriel Valley,
los indocumentados speak in whispers
and drift like the wind. . .

Papa tells mama not to cry.
Papa points to a crucifix eternally gorgeous
and begs mama not to cry.

Is there a place to hide
where the morning sun won't give them away?
I don't know,
but keep the boy quiet with a pretty song:

Ay, ay, ay, ay, canta y no llores
porque cantando se alegran cielito lindo los corazones.

De la sierra morena, cielito lindo, vienen bajando
un par de ojitos negros cieltio lindo de contrabando.

Ese lunar que tienes cielito lindo junto a la boca,

No se lo des a nadie cieltito lindo, que a mí me toca.

Ay, ay, ay, ay, canta y no llores
porque cantando se alegran cielito lindo los corazones.

Hearts swim like pretty fishes in the little boy's dreams.

But what can dreams do for him when dark clouds undulate,
like serpents, in a California sky?

Cry, cry, cry, no one will hear a thing.
In the land of plenty, no one hears anything.

Los mojados fade in another dumb and silent twilight.

Los indocumentados: Undocumented Mexican immigrants. **Operation Wetback, 1954:** A 1954 federally sponsored operation to apprehend and deport undocumented Mexican immigrants. Approximately 1.1 million los indocumentados were deported during the operation. ***Ay, ay, ay, ay, canta y no llores:*** Mexican folk song, "Cielito lindo." **Los mojados:** Literally, "wet ones" or "wetbacks;" undocumented Mexican immigrants.

María Elena dreams of Cuauhtémoc

       I dreamed
I married Cuauhtémoc
on a day when no deaths
were recorded in the empire.

I married Cuauhtémoc
on a Yucatán beach
in the middle
of the night / in the middle of a blues song.

Cuauhtémoc (my darling) pressed his hands against the sun,

burned the moon against the magpie,

let incense smoke in the heart,

brought wind and stillness into our souls.

I walked with Cuauhtémoc
through wet reeds,
unaccompanied by soldiers

sun sprinkled over cracked mahogany

ice become flame

drought become a merciful heart.

Cuauhtémoc: (Kwou-tem'ok) (1495?-1525) nephew of Motecuhzoma Xocoyotzin; Cuauhtémoc was the last great speaker of the Mexica empire, 1520-1525.

María Elena sueña de Cuauhtémoc

     Soñé
que me casé con Cuauhtémoc
en un día en el cual ninguna muerte
fue reportada en el imperio.

Me casé con Cuauhtémoc
en una playa de Yucatán
en medio
de la noche / en medio de una triste canción.

Cuauhtémoc (mi querido) prensó sus manos contra el sol,

quemó la luna contra la urraca,

dejó el incienso humear en el corazón,

trajo viento y quietud a nuestras almas.

Caminé con Cuauhtémoc
entre cañas mojadas,
desacompañada de soldados.

El sol saltó sobre caoba rajada

el hielo se convirtió en llama

la sequía se hace un corazón piadoso.

The last days of Señora Rodríguez

The stars flicker like ghost eyes
as Señora Rodríguez strings emeralds and colored lights in her kitchen
to ward off evil spirits.

All night long she searches the occult
to prophesy the next days,
      reading the stars to divine the fates.

In the morning,
Señora Rodríguez studies the sun through a prism of shadows.

She blows omens out her kitchen window.

Now, in her last days, the little bird of a woman
cranes her head from her front door.
She calls out to Jesus, her king.
Señora Rodríguez looks out among the fat, tail-finned cars,
searching desperately for her Savior.

She is surprised not to find him in her front yard
among clumps of crabgrass and smart-aleck crows.

Why should she be so disappointed?

Why does she close her door with such a heavy heart?

The last days of Señora Rodríguez: This poem takes place in 1960.

Pieces of the sun

Los Angeles, 1963.

A visceral poetry, half lament and half song,
textured, but amorphous,
sizzles and sighs along the rooftops and the points of stars
that bleed light,
like a liquid blanket over the City of Angels.

Where is God in this kingdom of freeways, violent light, and redundant death?

In the morning,
the prayers for redemption are often answered.

In the dawn comes revelation.

Poco and Esperanza sun themselves, like grapes,
in the iridescent fiery smog that dances densely above the metropolis.
They sit motionless, mute, dumb,
like two Mexica stone statues
crumbling into an immaculate, eternal silence.

Their two boys count ants that march mindlessly along cracked concrete.

Where are we heading, disabused of our myths,
disheartened and sacrilegious?

When did the sun first throw itself upon us sinners
in that initial, divine gesture of salvation?

Chávez Ravine, October 6, 1963

Today the Los Angeles Dodgers won the World Series.

Tonight there are celebrations from Chatsworth
to the Inland Empire.

And the stars on earth mingle
with those in heaven.

Horns honk like hoarse geese.

Fireworks explode, spasmodically, in the night,
bathing a cavalcade of cars
in a scintillating rainbow.

Far from the tumult,
a few ghosts gather in the ravine
and bow their spectral heads in sorrow.

---

a few ghosts gather in the ravine / and bow their spectral heads in sorrow: the Mexican-American neighborhoods of Bishop, La Loma, and Palo Verde in the Chávez Ravine area of Los Angeles were demolished in the 1950s to clear land for the construction of Dodger Stadium.

Archbishop Concepción preaches a theology of liberation along Highway 99

April 2, 1966.

These pilgrims have brought me to the Mother of Christ!

They have gently, but firmly, opened my eyes,
so that I see all kinds of wrong things
that I never noticed before.

I have become a sentinel whose heart
weighs heavy
as if it were ensconced in metal.

My mind is troubled with many pointed questions:

Why is there so much suffering
in a land of high-rises and supermarkets?

Why are there so many Christians in word only?
They do nothing truly to follow Christ's ministry.

They turn away from the Faith
which they so *heartily* say they embrace!

Yet the *heart* is measured by its works.

The keys to the Kingdom are given
to the truest prophets,
they who struggle righteously
for righteousness' sake.

We are mandated to do good works!
Christ demands it!

If we do not feed the hungry,

we have killed them.

We are reaching closer to the moon,
while we draw farther away from each other
on earth.

Archbishop Concepción: a fictional composite of many Roman Catholic priests and nuns who publicly aided César Chávez's United Farm Workers' strike. **These pilgrims:** Farm workers who made a 300-mile pilgrimage along Highway 99 from Delano to Sacramento California to ask Governor Edmund Brown, Sr. to call a special session of the state legislature to invest the farm workers with the same rights other workers had: a minimum wage, unemployment insurance, and the right to collective bargaining. They started on March 17 (St. Patrick's Day), 1966, with the goal reaching the California capital on Easter Sunday—to celebrate the Resurrection of Jesus Christ. At the head of the procession was a gold-embroidered banner depicting Nuestra Señora de Guadalupe, the patroness of Mexico. **If we do not feed the hungry, / we have killed them:** from a statement by Foulque de Neuilly (d.1202): "Feed the man dying of hunger, because if you have not fed him, you have killed him." **We are reaching closer to the moon:** a reference to the U.S. space program, specifically Project Apollo. Apollo XI landed on the moon on July 20, 1969.

Santa Ana canticle

August 20, 1968

¿Vienes conmigo a Los Angeles
y te quedas conmigo toda la tarde
mientras canto y te entrego mi corazón?

Yes, I could spend all day with you,
but I cannot find Los Angeles or Griffith Observatory.
I do not know where the Costa Mesa Freeway leads to.
I cannot tell you where you can find West Hollywood.

But that really doesn't matter all that much
because the moon has invited spirits
to pour indiscriminately over a treasure of hearts.

I can show you where you can find pastel colors
splashed all over daybreak in Santa Ana
and sweet brown honies wrapped in sunlight singing to the Virgin.

There are beautiful cats napping on South Evergreen Street
and sweet Chicano boys, whose hearts pound under their ribs,
singing in a sultry sundown: *"Para bailar la bamba
Para bailar la bamba se necesita una poca de gracia. . ."*

We could call up information
and find out where we can sing and dance like silly geese,
gallivant through the night till our hearts' content.

Maybe we can coax the spirits to glide down here,

where we could entertain them,
serve them ginger ale,
and make them giggle till dawn.

I bet if we sing long enough
we'd become jaguars prowling the Mexica kingdom
in the pouring rain.

¿Vienes conmigo a Los Angeles / y te quedas conmigo toda la tarde / mientras canto y te entrego mi corazón?: Will you come with me to Los Angeles /and spend the entire afternoon with me / while I sing and give you my heart? **Costa Mesa Freeway:** in Orange County, California. **South Evergreen Street:** in Santa Ana, California. The author lived on the 1800 block of South Evergreen Street as a boy, in 1968-1969. *"Para bailar la bamba / Para bailar la bamba se necesita una poca de gracia. . .":* lyrics from "La Bamba," a traditional Mexican folk song.

Four moons

South Vietnam, January 20, 1969.

As the Apollo astronauts flew over the moon's gray surface on Christmas Eve, they spoke to us of the beauty of earth—and in that voice so clear across the lunar distance, we heard them invoke God's blessing on its goodness.

In that moment, their view from the moon moved poet Archibald MacLeish to write: "To see the earth as it truly is, small and blue and beautiful in that eternal silence where it floats, is to see ourselves as riders on the earth together, brothers on that bright loveliness in the eternal cold—brothers who know now they are truly brothers."

    ★ PRESIDENT RICHARD MILHOUS NIXON,
        FIRST INAUGURAL ADDRESS, JANUARY 20, 1969

President Nixon's staccato voice floats upon the radio waves
like molecules of hot helium hissing
at the very nexus of life and death.

Small-arms fire crackles as the dusk bleeds into night.

The stars are only pieces of bent and jagged metal
that glow obliquely like souls submerged
in the sea of purgatory.

The Devil himself shoots up flares
announcing the reign of monsters.

President Nixon: Richard M. Nixon (1913-1994) thirty-seventh president of the United States, 1969-1974.

El lugar blanco

Winter 1970.

A million light years from Cauchichina,
soldados, with olive skin and bones hard as rock,
pray like cranes with heads bowed to the earth.

In that place, el lugar blanco,
el lugar de las garzas,
el lugar de las cañas,
the Mexica gods assemble,
descended from the forlorn moon,
to bless the world from edge to edge.

Our painted warriors press their prayers, like flowers,
into the ears of the gods,
who smile mischievously at the tremulous thought of love.

Cauchichina: in the sixteenth century, the Portuguese named Vietnam "Cauchichina," deriving "Cauchi" from "Giao Chi," the Chinese characters for Vietnam. **soldados:** Spanish, soldiers. **In that place, el lugar blanco, / el lugar de las garzas, / el lugar de las cañas:** Aztlán, the ancestral homeland of the Mexica people, also called the white place, the place of herons, the place of cranes. **the Mexica gods:** the deities of Mexica theology.

The blue lights

That neon half moon sinks in its vast, black sea.

The stars, our distant rulers, perched up in their icy thrones,
frown down upon us.

Their rule ends at dawn,
when our world, again, pirouettes beneath a new, watchful sun.

Love is the only truth, *singular and immutable.*
Love seasons our souls: *Oooo, what a little loving can do.*

In the morning, mechanical thunder rumbles in the heavens
from the engines of B-52s.

Five miles high the monstrous vultures clutch and hiss,
spilling fire and ice from their steel guts.

A napalm flash bleeds across the azure skies
like a UFO bending across dimensions,
or a Mexica god flaming in the ether.

Grenades explode. Helicopters burn,
sizzling down from the sky like dying dragons.
And the demons dance around the flaming gasoline,
singing the language of Hell.

A cholo from Studio City draws the deadly tarot card
as his carnales waste ten rice farmers outside Khe Sanh.
This sacred, soured blood is graffiti
splashed over an ancient horizon.

And the blue lights flash.

B-52s: U.S. bombers. **napalm:** chemical defoliant, used by the United States in the Vietnam War. **cholo:** a Mexican-American male. **carnales:** brothers, a term used among close friends. **Khe Sanh:** in South Vietnam.

Molecules of deep blue ice

A dispatch from Saigon, South Vietnam,
February 9, 1971.

Mercurio, Venus, Tierra,
Marte, Júpiter, Saturno, Neptuno,
Urano, Plutón, Vietnam.

Vietnam is another planet.
Its elliptical orbit freezes in the perpetual darkness.

A centrifugal force, bleak and overbearing,
drives the devils from their nests.
They gather, like flies, like lice,
around each sacrifice.

These demons will not be dispersed.

Our hearts are now only molecules of deep blue ice;
they are tempered by silence as old as space,
as remorseless as time.

Memories flicker, like dying light.

These sacrifices are unbrookable.

All of our angels have fled.

---

unbrookable: unbearable; insufferable.

El Miercoles de Ceniza

Easter Season 1972

The mystics and propagandists proclaim either the Kingdom come,
or the end of days.

But their forecasts are nothing more than a passing rain.

And we are no better for the language
they've put down at our feet.

So look toward the grunts,
huddled like a Diaspora under darkened skies:
Ángel, Jesús, Sgt. Ramírez, Rafael,
Chickie, Cali, Flipper,
El Dopy, Guardapedos,
Kekito, Pepsi Joe, Panchie,
Toro, Tacho, Neto.
They will tell you all you need to know.
The truth is the truth
no matter from whose mouth it comes.

Numbers mean nothing here.
No calculus can measure devotion.
And the atheists have a grim tablet upon which to write.

Only they who revere ash and burn the effigies
will lose themselves in eternity.

El Miercoles de Ceniza: Ash Wednesday. During the Easter cycle, Mexican-American Catholics consider their relationship to God and the Earth, especially on Ash Wednesday, when they publicly profess their adoration of the Christian faith. The Easter season is especially important because it reminds the faithful of the suffering Christ and his sorrowful Mother. The observance of Holy Thursday (El Santo Dolor del Huerto) recalls the agony and betrayal of Christ in the garden of Gethsemane. Good Friday is the holiest day of the year as Christians lament the three falls of Christ in the service La Procesión de las Tres Caidas as well as the Crucifixion itself. Mexican-American Catholics also recite Christ's seven last words, Las Siete Palabras—"Into your hands I commend my spirit"—as he died on the Cross. The solemn observation includes condolences offered to the Blessed Virgin Mary in a tradition known as El Pésame a la Virgen (The Sympathy, or Condolence, for the Virgin). The celebrations of Holy Saturday and Easter Sunday are joyous as the faithful anticipate the Resurrection of Jesus Christ. **grunts:** slang, infantrymen in the U.S. military, especially in the Vietnam War. **The truth is the truth / no matter from whose mouth it comes:** a reflection of the words of St. Thomas Aquinas: "The truth is the truth and proceeds from the Holy Ghost, no matter from whose lips it proceeds." **Only they who revere ash and burn the effigies:** On Easter Sunday, Mexican-American Catholics conduct a procession highlighted by the burning of an effigy of Judas Iscariot and the reunion of Christ with his Mother. **will lose themselves in eternity:** a reflection of the Chinese poet Li Po's words: "How many years since these valley flowers bloomed / To smile in the sun? / And that man traveling on the river, / Hears he not for ages the monkeys screaming? / Whoever looks on this, / Loses himself in eternity; / And entering the sacred mountains of Sung, / He will dream among the resplendent clouds."

North Hollywood, 1971

With burnt orange and ashen dahlia,
the quiet Mexican, native of Oaxaca, paints the last dreams
swirling across his last nights.

Those final visions churn furiously,
like birds blown across the heavens
in a great storm.

For years,
he has rubbed moon and rain
on his desolate canvasses.

He has worked unattended, like a monk,
within the walls of his sanctuary.

What exquisite art has blossomed, unnoticed,
among his glorious debris.

The splendor of his bespangled, metallic poetry
glimmers like a seascape
in the eyes of his many cats.

He stands, a last time, forlorn among the bits and pieces,
the relics,
the works of his life.

Tonight, the old man is washed away,
leaving his sacred heart among the broken clocks, bottles,
copper wire, crumpled metal, and orphaned cats.

North Hollywood: in southern California. **Oaxaca:** (pronounced: wa-ha'-ka) a state in southern Mexico.

A Mexican woman

North Hollywood, California, November 4, 1971

A Mexican woman leaves Archie's Ranch Market,
walking up Lankersheim Boulevard.

She hugs her bag of groceries to her chest,
like a treasure.

This Lady ignores the stores full of television sets and jewelry.

Something else glitters in her eyes.

Who is this woman, with the brown face
and head crowned with a bouquet of bundled hair?

Perhaps she is Tonantzin, come into our age
to protect us from so many demons that shamelessly wheel around us each day.

Lankersheim Boulevard: in North Hollywood, California. **Tonantzin:** in Mexica theology, the mother of the gods, who was worshiped as "our Venerated Mother."

The wounded Pegasus

Reseda, California, April 2, 1974

The Pegasus loosens itself, at last, from the weathered tin,
and plunges to the cracked cement.

It sits there, a long while, stuck and dumbstruck,
like an ant submerged in alcohol or in lime.

What viscous dreams of the metropolis ramble like radio waves
in the mind of the ancient, winged horse?

The traffic along Reseda Boulevard starts and stops like a fever.

The artificial lights of the Valley
swirl like the rings around Saturn.

Everything is artificial here.

A lone dying man notices the birdlike horse
collapsed and startled on the sidewalk.

The blind and old and dying man and the broken and forlorn Pegasus
bloom like the magenta flower
before both rise like balloons
toward the open evening sky.

The Pegasus loosens itself, at last, from the weathered tin: the Pegasus, the winged-horse, and the logo on a Mobil Oil Company tin sign. **Reseda Boulevard:** in the San Fernando Valley, Los Angeles County, California. **the magenta flower:** a fictitious flower of great beauty and fragrance.

The songs of raucous birds

Our poets see a new sun rising from the songs of raucous birds
and the scent of gnarled flowers.

They alone mine gold from dust.

Who else will make or lose the days to come?

Only poets invent the future.

Time ticks, ticks, ticks
as the sun comes and goes.

The sparse starlight, jagged and jarred,
suspended in the bronze, stifling ether
crowns the suburban sprawl with a heavy, ghostly peace.

The misfits among us court lovers and prayer-makers.
They enthrall hopeful kings
and find, in the end, that beauteous peace
the proud seldom know.

The freeways wander around and around

Chepe sings in los cantónes de jacinto
with his head craned toward the rays of the sun.

He darts through the kingdom,
a meteor dancing among ancient stars and the emerald eyes of saints.

For a fleeting moment he is free
and all that is heartache in East Los turns to starlight.

But dreams fade in the morning light
and at daybreak, the short side of nothing still adds up to nothing.

Chepe looks for a way out, but the pelo rojo and the cops
and los vatos gachos and los gabachos
and the tall, dumb buildings that throw long shadows on the heart
have a heavy toll to take.

The freeways wander around and around,
concrete ribbons decorating the City of Angels in a stark beauty, a breathtaking
    ugliness.

The headlights and taillights glimmer in liquid light.

The cars swim along in exquisite sadness.

There is no off ramp to the Promised Land.

---

los cantónes de jacinto: the houses of hyacinth. Cantón is slang for house. **East Los:** slang abbreviation for East Los Angeles. **pelo rojo:** marijuana. **los vatos gachos:** the mean (or bad) dudes. Gacho is a slang word. **los gabachos:** gringos or Anglos.

All the shiny things

The spirits of Mejicles fly around
with shiny things.

East Los is a placid sea of starlight and divine signs.

But Ysmael can't see the deities and the topaz moon
through the glare of graffiti
and electric lights.

Above the wail of police cars,
he can't hear Nuestra Señora sing to el niño Jesús.

The relentless hum of the freeway drowns out
la música de la raza and the heartbreaking cries for love.

Mejicles: slang for México. **East Los:** slang name for East Los Angeles. **Nuestra Señora:** Our Lady of Guadalupe, the Blessed Virgin Mary. **el niño Jesús:** the baby Jesus. **la música de la raza:** the music of the (Mexican) race (culture).

¿Qué ondo?

No, ese, L.A. ain't never gonna be the kingdom.
The cops and gabachos got their hands on everything
that's worth anything.

I'm tellin' you, mi carnal, they've been too smart for us.
We gotta think now, Chepe.

We gotta do what we gotta do.

I've been tellin' you, man, that pelo rojo in Woodland Hills
has got our names written all over it.
Hey, it's gotta be worth at least two grand.
C'mon, Chepe, we can dust them gringos locos no sweat.

We can get down to the valley in no time.
It's two o'clock.
There ain't no one on the freeways now.

How much you think we can get sellin' that grass
to the cholos in Los Nietos?

¿Qué ondo?: slang, What's up? **ese:** dude. **gabachos:** gringos or Anglos. **carnal:** brother. **pelo rojo:** marijuana. **Woodland Hills:** In the San Fernando Valley in southern California. **two grand:** two thousand dollars. **gringos locos:** crazy Anglos. **Los Nietos:** a community near East Los Angeles.

A freeway of fools

Ysmael and Chepe have a master plan.

They talk about it everyday.
These boys don't dream of anything else.

Their hearts flutter as they gaze into the days to come.

They've got it all figured out.

And they don't take advice from anyone.

Ysmael and Chepe drive down a freeway of fools.

There are many things to be known under heaven

No one knows what swirling visions
Chepe and Ysmael see in the crystal ball.

Who knows what voices they hear,
urging them towards the brink.

I don't know what the bystander can do
to turn these boys toward Zion.

All I know is that Ysmael and Chepe
are sliding down the freeway
and nothing will ever be the same.

La ascensión de San Gabriel

Gabriel "Chepe" Machado, 1982-2001

How many times did gorgeous angels dance
in Gabriel Machado's eyes?
        How many hearts fluttered
at his smile?

        Gabriel breathed beauty, brought heaven
to East L.A.,
so that cholos and chicas alike thought
that they had banished dark clouds forever
from the skies of the barrio.

But clear skies color only dreams in blue
while los comerciantes de muerte dance, brazenly,
through the neighborhood.

The sounds of gunshots ring in the ear forever.

Gabriel Machado's blood danced free
from the body,
        sparkling in the sun;
his eyes still beautiful, but lifeless,
like stained glass.

On the Feast of the Resurrection,
his body was given back
to the earth.

At sunset, San Gabriel, newly risen,
danced among the cumulus.

La ascensión de San Gabriel: Spanish, The ascension of St. Gabriel (into Heaven). **cholos:** dudes; sometimes gang members. **chicas:** young women. **los comerciantes de muerte:** the merchants of death; or, dealers in death; in this case, drug dealers. **Feast of the Resurrection:** Easter Sunday.

El Día de los Muertos

Los Angeles, November 2, 2001

The moon is dancing high above the cemeteries.

There is no grieving among the crosses.
No lamentation. But celebration.

Among these resting places, the ghosts thrive.
Skeletons strum guitars. They play ancient corridos
that tell histories of love and war.

Here México is no mere memory.
Here the dead are not dead.

Tonight, at this reunion of souls,
our ghosts thrive on tortillas, corn, and Coca-Colas.

Here, in this place,
Quetzalcóatl and La Virgencita bring us a sweet solace that knows no end.

El Día de los Muertos: The Day of the Dead, celebrated every November 2. On that day, Mexicanos in the United States and Mexico prepare food, drinks, and religious icons for their loved ones who have passed away. In many instances, the gifts are taken to the graves themselves. It is a joyous celebration, as the Mexican celebrants understand clearly that in remembering their loved ones they are keeping their memories alive and vibrant and that, in time, there will be a permanent reunion of souls. **Quetzalcóatl:** Mexica feathered-serpent god. **la Virgencita:** The Blessed Virgin Mary. The suffix "-cita" signifies endearment.

It's just a matter of time

★ *For Chepe and Ysmael,*
and all the Mexican-American boys who ache for the fire

How do I pull you boys from darkness,
and salvage your handsome beauty
that makes Our Blessed Mother weep?

How much should I feel? How much should I try
to reach inside your hearts?

Tell me why the violence is always brighter
than the peace of the Kingdom.

Why do you boys hunt fire day after day,
night after every night?

It can't keep going on this way.

All of you know you can't go on this way.

How much love can you show?
Can you come take my hand as we walk away from the wreckage?

I'm going to save you boys.
I'm going to save each and every one of you.
It's just a matter of time.

The Queen of the Angels visits East Los in a dream

The boys in East Los sing haunting songs
in the Blessed Virgin's dreams.

In her dreams, these boys turn dead flowers into poems
that ache with sweet sorrow.

Before she wakes, the Queen of the Angels touches each boy,
kissing them,
as if they were roses or rosaries.

---

the Queen of the Angels: the Blessed Virgin Mary. **East Los:** East Los Angeles.

213

L.A. will be red, white, and green again,
un metrópoli mexicano.

The world's gonna turn upside down
& it'll sure look better that way.

Our Holy Mother will walk down these streets
singing to her children in Spanish.

The flowers themselves will sing!

And we're gonna laugh till it hurts.

This time,
El Pueblo de Nuestra Señora la Reina de los Ángeles del Río de Porcíuncula
will be Mexicanos for keeps.

213: area code for East Los Angeles. **red, white, and green:** the colors of the Mexican flag. **Nuestra Señora:** Our Lady of Guadalupe, the Queen of México. **El Pueblo de Nuestra Señora la Reina de los Ángeles del Río de Porcíuncula:** The Town of Our Lady the Queen of the Angels by the River of the Little Portion; original Spanish name for Los Angeles. The Spaniards founded Los Angeles in 1781.

The continuing story
of Guadalupe
and Quetzalcóatl

Into the blueness, softly

mmmmm, darling, you're not
the woman of his dreams

no baby

he'll take another woman into his arms

play her love songs

play her some cool jazz

he plucks up women
like wildflowers

they bloom

only

for awhile

in the furious ice
of his heart

Guadalupe takes Line 42 downtown

She has 8 dollars and 93 cents
to buy something for her children.

Lupe's not going to buy taffy,
not chocolates;
naw, she's going to pick out something special
at El Tienda Grande de Jésus,
for her children to keep and say Mamá *gave us this*.

Maybe she'll buy a woolen blanket,
or beads,
perhaps a piñata,
or the statues of San Francisco de Assisi and his animals.

Lupe wraps gifts awfully pretty.

Maybe Lupe will get bold

Lupe takes off her head rag;
she's sick of it.
She says, "I want my hair in beads.
I'd look bold and sassy
with my hair done up like that,
but my hair is like wild Mexican wind
which I cannot bead.

I remember Gramma
used to bead Mamita's hair.

Gramma said how Mamita
looked fine
like some Mexica princess.

Yes my Mamita's pretty.

How I love her,
though I haven't seen her lately. . .

Elena,
girl, have you seen my
husband? Where's he been
staying? Maybe
some day I will be bold
with him."

Lupe didn't taste honey

Lupe heard no mariachis

There were no palpitating Mexican rhythms
leaping
down
6th Street
as he
pressed up
against her

Lupe didn't taste honey as he forced
his mouth
on her mouth

There wasn't any taste
of sweet lemon drops

No violets or forsythia
      blossomed
from her tears.

When the sky falls

Lupe saw the sky come crashing down this morning
when her husband's point of view
became a fist.

Well, yes, it gets pretty loud when the sky falls
so Miss Birdie, next door, called the cops.

The police came and wanted to take the husband downtown,
but Lupe didn't know where he was.

Lupe said she's sick of the time bomb,
she's tired of the screaming.
"I cannot live like this!"
So she signed a complaint against her husband;
she pressed charges.

The cops said: "You better get a restraining order
to keep him away."

Well that maybe all well and good,
but how does a restraining order
keep away the fear?

Our Lady of Guadalupe sings to the woman spirit

Our Lady of Guadalupe has the moon
in her hands.

She prays for women gone mute
by beating.

She hands them pieces of shimmering stars.

But scar tissue doesn't sing songs of tenderness,
roots of hair cannot dance dried in blood,
lips split open cannot kiss.

There are wounds that won't heal.

Our Lady washes the hearts of battered women in the river.

All night long she has been washing hearts:
leap of blood: blood-to-blood:
water to water:
and the river is old and rich
with the tears of women.

Lupe takes care

Lupe's not waiting for a revolution at dawn

She's not waiting for an exquisite poem
to be scrawled on some wall

No, she's not counting
on a phoenix purring in the fire

Lupe's just wondering if the sunrise
will ever bring her peace

Lupe dreams

Lupe washes her face,
says,
        "Sometimes I think
I'm not in East L.A.

Sometimes I'm in Havana,
sometimes Zion.

Maybe I'm in Spanish Harlem:
        out on Convent Avenue
drinking Coca-Colas
with some sweet man
and we're just sitting there
singing the blues
and wasting our time. . ."

Billie Holiday firma un autógrafo

—for *Billie's admirers in Spanish Harlem*

Alguien le da a Billie una rosa de tallo largo y un beso.

Alguien le da una Coca-Cola.

La lúz de la luna esta pesada esta noche.

Billie, estoy pensado en tí como tu me embromas
y despúes te vas,
forzando tinieblas.

¿Regresarás del eclipse?
Salpicastes con azulado
y silencio,
un reino trenzado en tu cabello, tú *(sensual)* enduciendo,

dándome besos clandestinos,

dándome ese poema
en tus ojos.

Billie Holiday: (1915-1959) cantante de jazz. The English translation follows: "Someone gives Billie a long-stemmed rose & a kiss. / Someone gives her a Coca-Cola. //Moonlight is heavy tonight. // Billie, I'm thinking of you: how you *tease me* & then go away, / forcing darkness. // Are you coming back from the eclipse? // You splashed with azure & silence, / kingdom braided in your hair, you *(sensuous)* enticing, // giving me clandestine kisses, // giving me that poem / in your eyes."

Lupe's geography

Lupe's geography sometimes
is broken glass,
broken
fire,
in a country barely whole.

But Lupe's not likely to give up that sweetness
that stings in her heart like bumblebees.

Lupe's not too likely
to turn her back on the sunrise.

Lupe's got some gumption!

Lupe, raised in a broken peace,
estranged from the Kingdom,
has always been near flame.

She's got some idea, new, keen,
about how she's going to innovate,
improvise. . .

mmm, she's gonna pull something really pretty
out of the ashes.

I hear Quetzalcóatl crying from behind the kitchen door

Quetzalcóatl burns the devil in effigy,
then crouches down
with the sad guacamaya
to write a prayer in the dirt.

Fifteen gods swarm in his brain like ants,
but poor Quetzalcóatl, he has a whole desert
in his heart and loneliness is eating into his bones.

A narcissus blooms in his hand.

He offers the blue moon to the Holy Ghost,
puts another wish in his heart,
and lies down on the cold and lonesome kitchen floor.

Quetzalcóatl: one of the most important Toltec and Mexica gods was Quetzalcóatl (pronounced: Keht-sahl-coh'-atl), whose name means the feathered snake, or, the plumed serpent. In this and the following poems, Queztzcóatl is in illegal alien in Los Angeles County. **gucamaya:** macaw.

Poor Elena's dream

I thought for sure I was holding
Quetzalcóatl's hand when the Police
opened the john door
and saw us on the floor
among the wilted gardenias, syringe, and horse
Course they didn't say anything
cause what can they say anyways
when we're sitting there already past Friday night
and it doesn't matter that we can't remember
what songs it is we're supposed to be singing
See little by little
Quetzalcóatl and me have gotten ourselves numb
and you don't need to guess how
Besides it's not like the disciples confided in us
any great secrets: *Well we were never much good
at carrying the weight of the world anyways*
but that doesn't matter much neither
cause Lady Day brought us something for the pain
so tell the Police to shut the damn door
we wanna turn out the light. . .

---

horse: slang for heroin. **Lady Day:** Billie Holiday (1915-1959) one of the greatest singers in jazz history; she suffered from an addiction to heroin.

Quetzalcóatl visits the neighborhood in a dream

The moon blooms. The moon comes and goes. . .

Quetzalcóatl dreams in soft turquoise
and magentas.
      His dreams are brushed
in sky blues and bright reds,
and colored in Náhuatl,
      sometimes Spanish;
but his dreams
never
get
painted
in English.

Quetzalcóatl's an illegal alien,
lying low
      in East L.A.,
a shadow to the I.N.S.

Quetzalcóatl finds some sweetness
in the barrio among la gente,
los vatos,
la raza: Quetzalcóatl cruises 3rd Street
with the low riders.

The street bends and sighs with the low riders driving
slowly and haltingly through the soul of the city.

Cholos break bread with Quetzalcóatl.
They dance on hot stones,
and pray,
      then cut out the heart of the barrio,
and hold it up to the sun. . .

Quetzalcóatl mines the sunset for gold dust and peace.

He picks in the moonlight for heaven,

but finds only shadows.

Quetzalcóatl holds a barren moon
in his hands.
A dying sun dances on his head.
He sucks at the root of bitterness
when all he wanted to do was dance.

And storm clouds fill his handsome head.

Náhuatl: language of the Mexica. **I.N.S.:** Immigration and Naturalization Service. **la gente:** the people. **los vatos:** the dudes. **la raza:** the Mexican race, or culture. **Cholos:** gang members in the barrio.

Everything's going to be better

No lilacs bloom on Soto Street,
but in the dazzling chaos of the City of Angels,
alchemists turn stone to starlight.

Tachito, Ñoño, Peanut, and Hipolito,
low-riders from Pico Rivera,
take Quetzalcóatl on a cruise through the city's throbbing heart.

Los cholos drive through L.A., the glorious jail,
riding slowly and *slower* from reality to dream.

Their faces glow in the holy light of headlights,
their heads undulate in the throbbing bass.

Cops nod as they swim by in their black and whites,
buildings melt,
and women fade to moonlight.

A visceral beauty burns in the Valley
as Ñoño's Impala glides along the Hollywood Freeway.

Auras of resplendent light dance in thin air above the Sepúlveda Basin,
and ghosts glide in the skies over Van Nuys.

In Reseda Park, 'Coatl and the low riders give girls tenderness
and pieces of the moon.

These boys are prophets.
They know all there is to know.
They laugh, without smiling, and say, *¡Todo será major!*

Pico Rivera: in Los Angeles. **the Valley:** the San Fernando Valley, in Los Angeles County. **the Sepúlveda Basin. . .Van Nuys. . .Reseda Park:** in the San Fernando Valley. **'Coatl:** Quetzalcóatl. **¡Todo será major!:** Everything's going to be better.

Quetzalcóatl is homesick

Quetzalcóatl's eyes are full of rain. . .

He's homesick for Teotihuacán.

He aches for home.

Quetzalcóatl's a heartache
for the Pyramid of the Moon,
the blood of martyrs,
and boundless ears of corn.

He can almost bury himself
in the red, sacred earth of México.

Quetzalcóatl can just about see
    the water spirits
        dancing
through fire at Capultitlán, La Venta, Tres Marías.

He can almost dream a new sun
and a rabbit hurled across the face of the moon.

Teotihuacán: Mexica city called Place of the Gods, twenty-five miles northeast of Mexico City. **Pyramid of the Moon:** at Teotihuacán. **Capultitlán, La Venta, Tres Marías:** cities near Mexico City.

What might have been

And Quetzalcóatl dreamed he was dying.
He dreamed his soul was rising up through the rusted smog,
over the Inland Empire and the Salton Sea.

And he dreamed he was free.

And as he was flying
he could see California sailing out far to sea.

And then he was laughing.

And as he was soaring over the New World,
he left a wake of fire blinding kings and devils.

What might have been: This poem was inspired by Paul Simon's 1974 song "American Tune."

Los cánticos y tristeza

Quetzalcóatl bursts out of the drought,
     breaking free from the eclipse.
He dives into distant horizons showered in sunrise
         and sugar tears,
swimming in a sea of broken light and lighted faces.

Quetzalcóatl dances in the blue light
of los cánticos y tristeza of the garment district
in Downtown L.A.,
El Pueblo de Nuestra Señora la Reina de Los Ángeles.

     He weeps with la gente obrera
         que no le escucha,
             praying to Jesús Cristo
     in a Spanish that smarts on the tongue.

Quetzalcóatl smolders with los trabajadores
sweating and bleeding in Oxnard sugar beets.

He eats raw starlight with the refugees,
who carve their names into the rusted rainbow.

Quetzalcóatl has heaven in central California,
where angels chew Chiclets
and sing La Bamba in the lettuce and turnip fields,
and hold La Purísima like they hold the sun.

---

los cánticos y tristeza: the songs / and sorrow. **El Pueblo de Nuestra Señora la Reina de Los Ángeles:** the Town of Our Lady the Queen of the Angels; the official name of Los Angeles, California. **la gente obrera / que no le escucha:** the working people / that no one hears. **los trabajadores:** the workers. **los refugiados:** the refugees. **La Purísima:** The Pure One, Nuestra Señora de Guadalupe.

Quetzalcóatl shoos the ghosts from the barrio

In the sudden downpour,
Quetzalcóatl washes his matted heart.

Images swirl out of the Bible
as the moon absorbs every sound from the earth.

Quetzalcóatl shoos the ghosts from the barrio.

He offers Nuestra Señora a blue rose
and a silent prayer:

"Santa María, I have dreamed of you every night for a year.
I have wanted to see you,
        to eat chile con carne with you,
to hear the sacred words dancing on your lips.

I have been so lonely.

Oh, merciful Mother,
send a lover to find me now,
to whisper sweet nothings in my ear."

Quetzalcóatl and Lupe

Quetzalcóatl's in love,

he's a lovebird for Lupe.

He just bought her a new dress;
he's gonna take her out dancing in the blue light of midnight;
they'll go *swirling* along a trail of starlight.

Quetzalcóatl gives Guadalupe his heart.

He's emptied the world of everything,
except her.

Quetzalcóatl loves Lupe.
Oh, and she loves him.
The loveliest blood shapes their hearts.

You watch,
Quetzalcóatl won't be here much longer.

He's gonna climb over the wall,
he's gonna make it to the other side.

He's gonna take Lupe away. . .

Cause of you

*Words should paint the color of a sound, the aroma of a star;
they should capture the very soul of a thing.*

★ RUBÉN DARÍO [1888]

You don't have to speak English
any language would do
actually you don't need to
say anything at all
and I'd still know
how much you love me

cause of you I've got the whole horizon
covered up in violets and
forsythia

    cause of you I'm scattering palm fronds
all over the dusk

cause of you
I've got hurricanes
dancing in my hands

Perseguida

Regresa del desierto,
hermosa mujer.
Encuentra los huacales de miel
y palabras suaves
que he dejado afuera
para tí.

Encuentra paz, toma la paz en tus manos.

Y cuando hayas regresado a casa
te darás cuenta
que no he dejado de amarte.

No he parado de cantar.

Perseguida: Pursuance. The translation of this poem into English follows: Come back from the desert, / beautiful woman. / Find the bowls of honey / and soft words / I've left out / for you. // Find peace, take peace in your hands. // And when you've come home / you will realize / I have not stopped loving you. // I have not stopped singing.

I've got enough love potion
to fill the Los Angeles River

Darling let's you & I dance down César Chávez Avenue after dark
after the lights go out in the Catholic Church
I bet all the cholos would turn out
just to watch us
shake down the moonlight
and the honies they'd be
out there too
making it to the r & b sounds
happy wasting their time
with us
oh darling I've got this 4-leaf clover says
you'll walk with me
down where the barrio glistens
with the wet rock 'n roll riffs
where the welfare mothers seem lovelier than poetry
aw Sweetness I can be your lover man
I can make myself
irresistible
oh come to me delicate with your mystery
come wet like honey
like music
I am the man
who wants to get lost
in love for you
I am the man
who's got clouds in his eyes for you
can't see
nothing but you
I wanna lead you
on to some greater love
to some greater
conclusion:

I've got Los Lobos wailing in my heart
& Billie Holiday's in there too singing some jazz for you
I have to know what you're hiding
oh be my soft refrain
my alto saxophone solo
my secret
just make yourself stunning
(I wanna live out a saga
on 3rd Street with you
where the ghetto glows
& the welfare mothers giggle at us
as we dance down every corner in East L.A).
I know a place we could sit
& wave to the cops
& just watch the traffic swim on by
we'll watch the boys blow dust
playing basketball
some of them running off somewhere to fight
we'll watch the welfare mothers just blend into the sunset
there is something so beautiful about our people tonight
they've left their beauty marks
all over the city
but I can't see no one but you
I'd love to hold you
on some rooftop
as the moonlight defines your face
as the world dances away
I am the man
who wants to get lost
in love for you
I am the man
who has these clouds in his eyes
for you:

I'm hanging on every breath
every possibility
I am the man
a lover in the barrio
holding on
for you

just holding on

César Chávez Avenue: in East Los Angeles, California. **Los Lobos:** Mexican-American band from East L.A. **Billie Holiday:** (1915-1959) U.S. jazz singer. **3rd Street:** in East Los Angeles.

Música para pigmeos

Mi alma es el color de índigo.

Mi alma es lodo suave.
Un oasis.

El alma es una puesta del sol.
Una luna, un miraje.
Una encrucijada.

Una ciudad entre la tierra y otro lugar.

Música para pigmeos: Music for pygmies. The translation of this poem into English follows: My soul is the color of indigo. // My soul is soft mud. / An oasis. // The soul is a sunset. / A moon, a mirage. // A crossroads. // A city between earth and some other place.

Nothing is as it was

Nothing is as it was, merely as it is remembered.
★ RAMÓN DEL VALLE INCLÁN

Goodnight princes and princesses,
the royal guardians of memory:
You have deserted us once more,
leaving us in the cold wind, uncomforted.

We remember only shades and shadows of the past;
nothing is clear, nothing sharp.

We recall the past when we want to recall it,
and how we want to recall it.

Everything that was is stored away,
all but forgotten,
in the treasure chests of our minds.

Ramón del Valle Inclán: (1866-1936) Spanish poet, playwright, novelist, and social critic. In his early career, Valle Inclán was influenced by the Symbolists; later he developed the genre of *esperpentos* (literally, grotesque sight, or absurdities, pieces of nonsense) to express visceral social criticisms. His novels included four *Sonatas* (1902-1905), particularly *Sonata de otoño* (1902), *Flor de santidad* (1904), the *Comedias bárbaras* including *Aguila de blasón* (1907), *Romance de lobos* (1908), *Cara de plata* (1923) *Tirano Banderas* (1926); *El ruedo ibérico* series as *La corte de los milagros* (1927), *Viva mi dueño* (1928) and poetry, including *Aromas de leyenda* (1907), *La pipa de kif* (1919), *Claves líricas* (1930), plays such as *El embrujado* (1913) and *La marquesa Rosalinda* (1913).

Christ smiles

Christ smiles and with little sweat raises the dead;
Tonatiuh turns envious,
      green as an avocado.

The Sun winks.

Tonatiuh: (pronounced: Toh-nah-ti-you) Mexica sun deity and lord of fate.

In the palms of our hands

Suddenly, love is irresistible.
Every prospect of love,
every remote chance for love
        dances
in the palms of our hands.

We'll blow the dust off our hearts
and revel, here, at the beginning of the rainbow.

Insinuations glow at dawn
as you and I paint hieroglyphs in the face of the moon,
and spirits search the skies for traces of sacredness.

My love is longer than an endless road.
It stretches out like arms yearning to embrace.

My poems are salvaged from shadows and moss and dark clouds.
They ache with tenderness.
They sing sweet refrains that can just about mend broken hearts.

These poems send electric shocks through languid moments
and sigh for make-believe kingdoms towering in tranquil dawns.

Isn't this where the kingdom begins?

We'll have skimmed the cream off the Milky Way / made a permanent ellipse by the yet unchartered tail of Halley's Comet.

★ NTOZAKE SHANGE

These houses are cluttered with ghosts and desire;
here, heartbeats sweep lovers off their feet,
and poems are tropical flowers and aphrodisia.

Spirits glide over the Santa Ana Freeway
in search of undiscovered suns,
inchoate prayers.

Isn't this where the kingdom begins?

Here, in Our Lady's city, lovers sigh,
nervously anticipating the rhapsody of love.

The sun blushes above us.

Everybody here is a lover.

Love seems to follow, wildly, the San Andreas Fault as it shivers
within the backbone of California.

Oh, Union Station is awash in lovers.
The garment district sings boleros of love.
Why, God himself is signing a capella,
momentarily lost in the mists of romance.

Oh, sweetheart, love is the panacea.
I've known this all my life.

Tonight let's get lost in love,
exploring nakedness and ancient memories,
here where the kingdom begins.

Our Lady's City: Los Angeles. The official Spanish name for the city is El Pueblo de Nuestra Señora la Reina de los Ángeles del Río de Porcíuncula (The Town of Our Lady the Queen of the Angels by the River of the Little Portion). **San Andreas Fault:** major earthquake fault line in California. **Union Station:** Railroad depot in Downtown Los Angeles.

The world leaves signs

The world leaves signs, unmistakable totems, in our hearts.

Lovers leave ominous clouds, dazzling colors,
where once their hearts dwelt.

What beautiful poems could we write
if only we could speak every language?

What exquisite phrases would tumble out of our hearts?

Would we have peace of mind if we could atone for our sins with songs?

Would we have solace at last
if the lovers who visit us in our dreams
could lead us into paradise?

Our lives are like clouds,
sculpted beautifully for a fleeting moment,
and then gone.

Mae C. Silverberg whispers to the poet in a dream

I heard my grandmother whisper my name.
She told me my ancestors are watching over me,
enthralled by the modern world,
and aching to see where my visions
will take me.

My grandmother said the sacred books reveal the light alive
at the beginning of the world,
where the birds of the only Zion sing
at the right hand of the Lord.

She said she knows how much I miss her
and she told me to keep hope,
for it shall lead me to my home.

And then Grandma said: "Don't lose faith, Anthony.
This separation will not last forever."

Mae C. Silverberg: (1900-2000) maternal grandmother of poet Anthony S. Koeninger (1960-). Mae Cohen Silverberg was born in New York City on April 2, 1900. She taught in the New York City public schools from 1927 until her retirement in 1970. She was an expert crossword puzzle solver and created highly acclaimed works of crochet and knitting. Mae C. Silverberg was a student of Jewish theology and U.S. history and literature. She was beloved for her compassion, gentleness, and selflessness. She died in Santa Barbara, California, on March 23, 2000, ten days short of her one-hundredth birthday. She was buried in Santa Barbara Cemetery.

Prayers for St. Rebecca

May the angels, dear Rebecca, take you into Paradise.
May the martyrs come to welcome you on your way
and lead you into the holy city of Jerusalem.

May the angels, dearest Rebecca, lead you into Paradise.
May the martyrs receive you at your coming.
May the Spirit of God embrace you.
May you receive eternal rest and peace.
> ★ ROMAN CATHOLIC FUNERAL RITE

Blessed are they that mourn: for they shall be comforted.
> ★ MATTHEW 5:4

My heart is a ship full of lead.
It's listing to starboard, taking on the sea.

Dearest Rebecca,
mother, councilor, protector,
my heart burns with sorrow and will smolder
until my last day.

Then, in the final moments,
the dreams and visions will bear the splendid fruit of your spirit.

Let the poems and flowers tumble away, the sun and moon too.
All beauty, on earth and in the sky,
is diminished by your presence.

So let that beauty be diminished, and the heart stop smoldering
when all earthly things for me pass away.

What is divisible from shadow?

How do I draw near the Kingdom,

where you are?

Will I decipher that knowledge kept in spectral hands?

Let the spirits come to me now
so that they flood my dreams,
crowding out the heartache and each bleak vision, like rain clouds,
that darken heart and soul.

Rebecca, Rebecca, your name is a prayer, a song,
the echo of a sigh.
The most beautiful birds, like soft, soft wind,
sing to you.

Visions of St. Rebecca swirl in my eyes.

I see you clothed in mauve and azure,
and crowned in sacred light.

Blessed Rebecca, patron saint of the emerald cities of Heaven,
keep me in your eyes.

Guide me along the paths that lead to your side.

St. Rebecca: Rebecca Ellen ("Beth") Koeninger was born in New York City on March 12, 1939, the daughter of Mae C. and Charles Silverberg. Her beloved father died in 1946, when Rebecca was just six years old. Her mother, who never remarried, raised her daughter with full and abiding love and wisdom so that the girl grew up to become a magnificent woman. After her graduation from Forest Hills High School in Queens, New York, in 1957, Rebecca attended Cornell University and Hunter College, where she earned her Bachelor of Arts degree in sociology. She went on to earn a teaching credential from Hunter. She had two children from her first marriage, Anthony Sean Koeninger (b. 1960) and Maria Elena Pastor (b. 1961). She moved to California with her two children on August 20, 1968. On September 3, 1969, Rebecca married her beloved second husband, Roger Milton Koeninger. A third child, Charles Roger Koeninger, was born in 1972.

After she completed her studies at Hunter College, Rebecca taught elementary school in predominantly Hispanic neighborhoods in New York City, Miami, and Santa Ana. In the early 1980s, Rebecca studied in the nursing program at Ventura College, where she received her nursing degree in 1981. She served for twenty-three years as a nurse, first at St. John's Medical Center in Oxnard and later at Atascadero State Hospital. She was widely acclaimed as a superior health care worker. From her high school years, beginning in 1954, until her death in 2005, Rebecca Koeninger studied Cuban, Chinese, and Japanese history. She was a student of Roman Catholic theology and socialist theories. In addition, she was active in the civil rights movement in the 1960s and 1970s and was a defender of animal rights. She enjoyed watching Brooklyn (later, Los Angeles) Dodgers baseball and listening to the Beatles. Her religious, political, and cultural values profoundly influenced her eldest son, Anthony.

Rebecca Koeninger died in Templeton, California on February 11, 2005, after a valiant struggle against leukemia only four months following her retirement from nursing. A devout Roman Catholic, Rebecca ascended into Heaven on February 11, the feast day of Our Lady of Lourdes, a day for all to give thanks and praise to the Blessed Virgin Mary who appeared to a poor girl in Lourdes, in southern France on February 11, 1858. The Blessed Mother told the girl, "I am the Immaculate Conception." The Shrine of Our Lady of Lourdes is a major pilgrimage center and it boasts holy, healing waters. The waters heal some pilgrims and all receive the grace of Our Lady of Lourdes. Rebecca Ellen Koeninger was a devotee of Our Lady of Lourdes. Thus, God raised Rebecca's soul into Heaven on the wonderful feast day of the ever merciful and compassionate Lady. She was preceded in passing by her grandmother and namesake, Rebecca Reiber (1934), her grandfather Victor Cohen (1948) and her beloved, beloved mother Mae C. Silverberg, who died ten days short of her one-hundredth birthday, on March 23, 2000. Her mother always referred to her daughter as "My darling Rebecca." Rebecca's mortal remains were cremated. Her ashes were interred a few yards away from her mother, Mae C. Silverberg, in Santa Barbara Cemetery in a plot which one day will also accommodate the ashes of her beloved son and best friend, Anthony Koeninger.

Rebecca Ellen Koeninger now rests in glory at the right hand of God and is showered in the grace and mercy of the Blessed Virgin Mary and Her Son, Jesus Christ, the Savior of humanity. Blessed Rebecca: Pray for us.

What can our poets tell us?

Our poets mark each revelation
with lament and hyacinth.

Are the poets among us the truest visionaries?
What do they know of past days, of this day,
and of what will be?
What can they tell us of our hurried and ephemeral lives?
What is revealed in their sullen yet beautiful poems?

Will their words give us a tragic shudder
in the days yet to come?

It's later than it seems

Once, it seemed, there was enough time
to explain to the Lord
how our lives would be holy,
how our dreams would lead us
onto the paths of righteousness.

Where is the hope, the exuberance,
that we were within reach of the Kingdom?

Why has that earlier hopefulness,
like a house of straw,
come down by the wolf's breath?

A trillion years from now

All the lines are down. The radio waves are still.
This is a perfect, melodic stillness,
an immaculate solitude under a soft, soft mauve sky.

The obelisks in our great cities glimmer
in their scintillation.

Even the faces of our dead glow like golden masks.

But each rainbow fades to a luminous shadow.
A resonant wind extinguishes the last fires
weeping in the sun.

All things are precipitate and hurried.
Everything is ephemeral, yet enduring.

A trillion years from now, what new race
will count itself blessed
among stars that do not now shine?

The moon wind

Audrey Hepburn has been gone now
for ten years and many months,
yet divinities with emerald eyes still reign
over the olive trees bending
in the moon wind.

All souls, like music and eternity,
chime in the clock of the world
as lights tumble in the sky
like forlorn wishes.

Taxes and tyranny butt themselves hard
against our hearts,
but tranquility, illumination,
as in moon slope,
bring paradise under turquoise skies. . .

Green, yellow fade to sunset,
but in love of faith we shall be blessed.
The sun will rise in Pisces sign
and you and I are loved by St. Rebecca,
who smiles at us among the Easter iris.

Audrey Hepburn: (1929-1993) elegant actress born in Brussels, Belgium and raised in London. Hepburn won the Academy Award for best actress for her performance in the 1953 film, *Roman Holiday*. She also had memorable roles in *Breakfast at Tiffany's* (1961) and *My Fair Lady* (1964). She served as a special United Nations UNICEF ambassador, a post she used to raise funds for impoverished children in Latin America and Africa. **The sun will rise in Pisces sign / and you and I are loved by St. Rebecca:** Rebecca Ellen Koeninger (1939-2005), the author's beloved mother. Pisces was Rebecca Koeninger's zodiacal sign.

The Gospel According to St. Rebecca

Revealed on November 4, 1960.

Because of something, something you saw or something you intuitively knew,
because there will be Some Thing for which you will love,
I prophesy to you when the stars are young.
Listen to me. Keep your mouth shut.

I tell you to forget kings.
A lone heron speaks enough for God.

The Lord does not withhold his wisdom,
but only those who seek it, *know it*.

The oil of catechumens is the oil of prophecy.
Blessed are they that are anointed,
for they shall see.

They shall know the heart of the Lady.

So fill your heart with grace, your hands with good works.

Be counted in the Faith,
burnished by the risen Christ, our sun, our moon.

St. Rebecca: St. Rebecca Ellen Koeninger (1939-2005). **Because of something, something you saw or something you intuitively knew:** Inspired by Gwendolyn Brooks's poem, "Leftist Orator in Washington Park Pleasantly Punishes the Gropers" (1960). **oil of catechumens:** holy oil used in baptism. **the Lady:** The Blessed Virgin Mary.

Goodnight noises everywhere

Goodnight magnificent city sparkling in the winter ether.
Your tall buildings—the temples of strange gods—
throw their flickering shadows
on men and machines, who stand bewitched
in the glare of neon and moonlight.

Who are these men and women whose tears daily
dance in the heart of the metropolis? Look at these people now,
with so little time before they are wiped off
into oblivion.

On a quiet night like tonight
you can almost hear the hum of souls
lifting upward.

What should I say to the ancestral ghosts
who crowd into my dreams
and tell me what might have been?

Goodnight ghosts.

Goodnight to all the noises that rumble and roar,
the noises that whir and purr.

Goodnight wondrous world, wicked world.
Now take my spirit home.

Goodnight noises everywhere: This line is from Margaret Wise Brown's 1947 children's book, *Goodnight Moon.*

The day after tomorrow

I'm gonna get up
and dance,
just rise like a phoenix dancing a resurrection dance. . .

With everyone watching,
I'm gonna dance like a bright phoenix,

    burning a hole through the night.

Anthony Sean Koeninger was born in New York City in 1960. Koeninger attended Santa Barbara High School, Santa Barbara City College, and the University of California, Santa Barbara where he received a Ph.D. in history in 1988. He is a professor of history at Cuesta College in San Luis Obispo.